MW01293735

ADVENTURES IN AMERICA

An Introduction to American History
For the Grammar Stage

WRITTEN BY:
ANGELA BLAU

Copyright

All contents copyright ©2017 by Angela Blau. All rights reserved.

No part of this document or the related files may be reproduced or transmitted in any form, by any means (electronic, photocopying, recording, or otherwise) without the prior written permission of the author. The author does give permission for the original purchaser to make photocopies of the student materials for use within their immediate family only.

Limit of Liability and Disclaimer of Warranty: The publisher has used its best efforts in preparing this book, and the information provided herein is provided "as is". Angela Blau makes no representation or warranties with respect to the accuracy or completeness of the contents of this book and specifically disclaims any implied warranties of merchantability or fitness for any particular purpose and shall in no event be liable for any loss of profit or any other commercial damage, including but not limited to special, incidental, consequential, or other damages.

Trademarks: This book identifies product names and services known to be trademarks, registered trademarks, or service marks of their respective holders. They are used throughout this book in an editorial fashion only. In addition, terms suspected of being trademarks, registered trademarks, or service marks have been appropriately capitalized, although Elemental History cannot attest to the accuracy of this information. Use of a term in this book should not be regarded as affecting the validity of any trademark, registered trademark, or service mark. Angela Blau is not associated with any product or vendor mentioned in this book.

Adventures in America

This program is intended for use with your kindergarten or early elementary student. Get ready for a year of adventure along with the brave men and women who built this country. From the Native Americans who first dwelt in the land, to the heroic Patriots who fought for liberty, to the pioneers who traveled from the towns and cities into the unknown, to legends about such "tall" heroes as Pecos Bill and John Henry, these stories will thrill and inspire your kindergarten or early elementary student.

Why use this guide?

You may be planning to do a four year chronological history cycle beginning in first or second grade. However, you may not want to wait until your child is in third or fourth grade before they learn the stories of significant people in American history, such as Christopher Columbus and George Washington. This program will expose your student to these important people and their stories, and will provide a great foundation for more detailed studies in future years.

What does this program include?

Inside this guide you will find stories to read to your child twice each week followed by review questions that will guide your student into the early skills of narration. Read Alouds are scheduled for you, and there is even a weekly guided study of each state using *Smart About the Fifty States*. In addition to the scheduled readings and review questions, there are also engaging hands-on crafts and activities each week, as well as suggested readers and picture books.

Do I need the Student Pages?

The Student Pages are sold separately and are necessary for creating a student notebook that will serve as a wonderful tool for reviewing your year of Adventures in America. Student Pages include coloring pages that relate to the week's reading, notebook pages for the States study, as well as spaces to record narrations and copywork.

What resources do I need?

Besides this teacher's guide, you will need the Student Pages, as well as the book *Smart About the Fifty States*. Below is a list of scheduled Read Alouds that you may wish to purchase or borrow from your local library. Related picture books are suggested as go-alongs for each week. If you have access to a good library, you should be able to locate these easily. If you are unable to borrow the titles or choose not to use these, that will not affect the program at all! They are simply provided for those who wish to supplement with additional titles. For your convenience, a list of materials needed for each week's crafts and activities is located at the back of this guide on page 144.

Read Alouds

For students who are ready to listen to chapter books with few or no pictures, I have scheduled ten books as Read Alouds. These will be read chronologically throughout the year and roughly correlate to the topics being studied. I highly recommend that you encourage your student to narrate after each reading. Ask questions such as, "What happened to (name of character) in this chapter?" to prompt them. Require your student to answer using complete sentences. This may take work in the beginning, but they will eventually become used to replying in this manner. It is perfectly fine for these narrations to be done orally only, however I have included templates that you may choose to use as notebook pages for recording the narrations once a week. These pages can be used to record narrations from Read Alouds, history or readers. Simply write down your student's narration on the lines provided. If your student is a reader, ask them to read it back to you. If they are fairly capable writers, you may wish for them to copy your model onto another paper. There is a space on these pages for your student to illustrate their narration with a drawing if they wish to do so.

Booklist:

Pocahontas and the Strangers (Bulla, Clyde Robert)

Squanto, Friend of the Pilgrims (Bulla, Clyde Robert)

A Lion To Guard Us (Bulla, Clyde Robert)

Tolliver's Secret (Brady, Esther Wood)

The Cabin Faced West (Fritz, Jean)

The Courage of Sarah Noble (Dalgliesh, Alice)

The Matchlock Gun (Edmonds, Walter D.)

Little House on the Prairie (Wilder, Laura Ingalls)

On the Banks of Plum Creek (Wilder, Laura Ingalls)

In Grandma's Attic (Richardson, Arleta)

Readers

If your student is a reader, you may choose to use this selection of Early Reader books that roughly correspond to the topics studied. These are scheduled every other week, giving you two weeks to complete each reader. Feel free to work through these books at your student's pace in the given order.

Copywork

There is an optional copywork sentence provided each week. If your student is ready to do this, copy the sentence onto handwriting paper to serve as a model for your student to copy from. If the sentence is frustratingly long for your student, break it up over two or even three days. They can copy into the student notebook pages, and use the blank space above either to illustrate the sentence or to glue a photo of the hands-on activity for that week.

Activities

Each week has one hands-on craft or activity, with detailed instructions provided. Some directly relate to the day's reading, while others are general crafts from the time period being studied. These range from very simple (using watercolors to make an American flag) to more involved (making fabric dye from berries). You decide whether to do all of them, or simply pick and choose those which you think would most interest your student.

Instructions for State Studies

You will be learning about one to two states each week. Read the scheduled pages in *Smart About the Fifty States*. Complete the notebook page for that state by filling in the required information and identifying the location of the capital. I suggest that you identify the capital with a foil star sticker, letting your student place it in position. You will also find an empty rectangle on each page. This space is for attaching a state flag sticker, which can be inexpensively purchased from many online venders or educational supply stores.

After this page is finished, turn to the blank US map and color that state. This is a perfect time to review the names, locations and capitals of previously studied states! By simply pointing to each state and saying its name and capital, your student will probably memorize them easily. You may also wish to create flashcards with the state name on one side and its capital on the other. Only use the flashcards for the ones already learned, adding more as you progress through the weeks.

Week 36 is scheduled as a "My State" project. There are no readings from the guide for that week. Instead, plan on checking out books and other resources from the library, or follow the internet links provided to learn more about your own state. **You may wish to celebrate at the end of this week with a party and showcase your student's work from the year to grandparents or friends.**

Table of Contents

Adventures in America Week 1

	Day 1	Day 2	Day 3
Reading	Read *Native Americans*	Read *Iroquois*	Read *Smart About* pg.15
Coloring/ Activity	Coloring Page, pg. 3	"Wampum Beads" activity	Color Delaware on the blank US map, pg. 2
Notebook	Narration from Read Aloud, history or reader, pg. 4	Copywork, pg. 5	Fill out notebook page for Delaware, pg. 6

Optional Read-Aloud:

Pocahontas and the Strangers

- Day 1: Chapter 1
- Day 2: Chapter 2
- Day 3: Chapter 3
- Day 4: Chapter 4
- Day 5: Chapter 5

Related Picture Books:

- *North American Indians* by Douglas Gorsline

Possible Reader:

- *Christopher Columbus*, Krensky

Activity: "Wampum" Beads

•Use air dry clay or the recipe below to form beads of varying sizes and shapes.

•Use a toothpick to poke a hole all the way through each bead. Air dry or bake in low oven.

•Decorate with paints. Talk about the possible meanings of different colors.

•String onto elastic string or yarn. You may wish to make a pattern. Tie a knot after the last bead.

•Wear as a necklace, bracelet or glue to a headband. Boys may want to make it into a belt or a sash.

Recipe for clay:
2 c. flour   1 c. salt
2 tablespoons oil   ¾- 1 c. water

Mix flour and salt, then add oil. Slowly add water until you have the right consistency. Once formed into shapes, bake in an oven at 250 degrees for one hour.

Optional Copywork: The wampum beads were valuable to the Iroquois people.

Note In some parts of this guide, I have used the name Native Americans to describe the first inhabitants of North America. In other parts, I have used the name "Indians." I do not intend or wish to offend anyone by this word. I am only using it because it is what was most often used by people during the time periods being studied, and I am attempting to be as true as possible to the actual events.

Notes

Native Americans

Long before white men landed their ships on the shores of North America, there were people who had been building homes and growing food in every part of the land. White men first named these native peoples "Indians," but now they are also called "Native Americans" or "First Nations People," to show that they were indeed the original inhabitants of the land we now know as America.

Nomadic tribes roamed the Great Plains, hunting the plentiful buffalo that grazed there. Different tribes built clay buildings in the Southwest. Others lived in the woodland forests of the East Coast, growing corn and other plants and hunting deer and fish for meat. Still more gathered food along the Northwest coasts. Almost every part of America had been inhabited since early history, and there were already rich cultures that had been developing over the years.

One very interesting and mysterious ancient culture built mounds all over the land. They piled up dirt to create different geometric shapes. Besides squares, circles and pyramids, there were also reptiles, birds and other creatures, all formed out of dirt. Some were as tall as three houses standing on top of each other! Today you can still see the Great Serpent mound in Ohio. It is twenty feet wide, three feet tall and wiggles its snake shape around for more than 1,000 feet! The serpent mound was not used to bury anybody, but there are other mounds that look like cones standing up from the ground that were used as tombs for important people. In some places, whole cities were built from mounds with a tall earthen mound wall surrounding them. Often buildings like homes were built right on top of the mounds.

For some reason, the culture of "mound builders" disappeared and people eventually forgot the stories about them. How did that happen? Those people did not use written language to record their stories. The only way to pass stories from generation to generation was through telling them over and over again. For example, a grandfather would tell his grandchildren and great-grandchildren about important happenings in their tribe. Stories of great hunts were often passed down this way, as well as tales about how battles were won against enemy tribes. Warriors who had fought bravely were remembered through the years. If the great-grandchildren forgot the stories or were unable to tell them to their own grandchildren, eventually there would be nobody alive who had any memory of those things. That seems to be what happened to the stories about the mounds. Since the stories have been forgotten, today there is not very much known about the people who built them or what happened to the builders.

However, the mounds do show us that there were ancient Native Americans who knew how to farm the land and grow food instead of just being hunters and gatherers. How does a mound of dirt tell us this? Hunters and gatherers were people who traveled around almost constantly. They never stayed in the same place for very long. After hunting in one area for awhile, there were not many animals or edible plants left. They would then pack up their wigwams or other portable houses and travel on to a new area with more plentiful game and food. Eventually, it would become harder and harder to find food in that area. Again, they would pack up their wigwams and journey on. But, the mound builders must have stayed in one place for a long period of time. Otherwise, they would not have had the time to complete their walled cities and elaborate mounds. The only way they could have done that was by learning to farm the land and grow their own food.

Review Questions:

1. What kinds of mounds did the mound builders build?
2. How were stories passed down through time by Native Americans?

Iroquois: Festival Day

Oneida fingered the string of beautiful shell beads that hung around her neck. The wampum beads were valuable to the Iroquois people. They could be used as money when trading for goods, were considered meaningful gifts for weddings and other special events, and they even told stories. White beads symbolized health or peace. Giving another clan a string of red beads was a summons to war. Oneida's own beads had been given to her by her mother as Oneida approached womanhood. They were her most prized possession.

Today, Oneida wanted to look her best. Her soft deerskin skirt was decorated with porcupine quills, beads and shining silver. On her head sat a beautifully beaded tiara. It was the first day of the year's biggest harvest festival. The "three sisters," or the three crops of beans, corn and squash, had grown strong and healthy. Now it was time to celebrate the bounty of life-giving food that the clan had worked so hard to grow. Oneida was grateful to have a rest from farming in order to play games, sing traditional songs and perform dances. In the Iroquois nation, the women were the farmers, while the men hunted, fished and went to war. Every man was considered a warrior, and there were frequent skirmishes, or battles, between the Iroquois and other tribes. All the men from the surrounding areas would attend the festival, wearing their colorfully feathered headdresses. Oneida's own father was known to be one of the bravest Iroquois warriors. He was a talented warrior, and the younger men revered his skills. To mark his high position in the tribe, his own headdress was especially large and intricately decorated with shining beads and perfectly arranged feathers.

Excitement buzzed in the air! The longhouse was filled with bustle and movement as hair was braided and adorned with feathers. Sixty members of the clan slept inside the longhouse together. The building was made of a long, rounded frame covered with bark. Inside was a raised platform, like an upstairs, used for sleeping. Mats and screens divided the house into sections, like rooms that provided a small amount of privacy. These buildings were built to last, unlike the teepees and wigwams used by other tribes. The Iroquois stayed in one village for about twenty years, and then moved on so the soil could rest after having been farmed for so long.

Stepping outside the longhouse, Oneida saw even busier preparations taking place. Bushels of herbs and berries sat next to baskets filled with different meat and fish for the meals. They would feast on wild turkey, deer and salmon along with the plentiful corn, beans and squash. With her mouth watering in anticipation, Oneida joined the action by helping to pound corn into flour. Laughter and singing filled the air, and her spirits soared as she looked forward to the week's events!

Review Questions:

1. Describe the houses of the Iroquois.
2. What were the jobs of the Iroquois men and women?

Adventures in America Week 2

	Day 1	**Day 2**	**Day 3**
Reading	Read *Christopher Columbus, Part 1*	Read *Christopher Columbus, Part 2*	Read *Smart About* pg.45
Coloring/ Activity	Coloring Page, pg. 7	"Make a Telescope" activity	Color Pennsylvania on the blank US map, pg. 2
Notebook	Narration from Read Aloud, history or reader, pg. 8	Copywork, pg. 9	Fill out notebook page for Pennsylvania, pg. 10

Optional Read-Aloud:

Pocahontas and the Strangers

- Day 1: Chapter 6
- Day 2: Chapter 7
- Day 3: Chapter 8
- Day 4: Chapter 9
- Day 5: Chapter 10

Related Picture Books:

- *Columbus* by Ingri & Edgar Parin D'Aulaire

Possible Reader:

- *Christopher Columbus*, Krensky

Activity: Make a Telescope

Materials:
- Paper towel roll
- Scissors
- Construction paper
- Glue
*Optional: Colored cellophane

• Take a paper towel roll and cut a piece of colored construction paper to fit around the roll. Decorate if desired.

• Glue the paper around the roll.

• If desired, attach a piece of colored cellophane on the bottom and secure with a rubber band, to see things in a new color.

• Have fun exploring with your telescope!

Optional Copywork: Christopher Columbus thought the world was round like an orange.

Note For Day 1's reading, you may wish to have a globe and an orange to demonstrate how the earth is round to your child.

Notes

Christopher Columbus, Part 1

Long, long ago in the country of Italy, a boy named Christopher Columbus had a brave new idea. Although scientists had long ago proven the earth is a sphere, many uneducated people still thought that the world was flat, like a piece of paper. If you roll a pencil across a piece of paper, it eventually falls off the edge. Some people even thought that if you sailed a boat far enough out into the ocean, your ship would also sail right off the edge of the world! For many reasons, most sailors stayed close to land, only sailing around the coasts. Not very many people had been brave enough to sail out into the wide, blue water.

One day, Christopher Columbus sat holding an orange in his hand. The more he looked at the orange, the more his idea made sense. Christopher Columbus knew that instead of being flat like a piece of paper, the world was actually round like an orange. If that was true, then there was no way a ship could ever fall off the edge. It also meant that you could travel any direction and if you kept going far enough, you would end up back where you started. His brave new idea was to sail west to reach east!

Others would just laugh at this strange idea and say that it couldn't be done, but that did not make Christopher stop thinking about it. Through all of his life, he would prove to be a man who would never give up!

When he turned thirteen, Christopher left home and went to sea. He loved sailing on the strong ships. He liked to breathe in the smell of the salty air and feel the spray of the water. He delighted in the adventures that he had as a sailor. One day while Christopher was out on the ocean in his own ship, he was suddenly overtaken by a fleet of pirate ships! Pirates were sailors who attacked other ships, stealing whatever was on board. Sometimes they stole the ships themselves; sometimes the ships would sink to the bottom of the ocean. Christopher Columbus faced the pirates and fought for his ship, but he could not save it. The entire ship and everything on it were lost as they sank into the water. Some people say that Christopher found an oar floating by and held on tightly. The oar carried him to land in a country called Portugal. Other people say that he swam the entire six miles to the coast and called it a "blessing of God" that he survived. Christopher was saved, but he had lost everything he had except his courage and his determination to sail to new places.

In Portugal, Christopher heard some exciting stories told by a group of sea-faring people called Vikings. There were stories of sailors who had sailed so far that they had come upon a huge mass of land across the Atlantic. He also met many Portuguese people who agreed that the world was in fact round. These stories inspired Christopher to continue believing his old dream that crossing the ocean was possible.

Review Questions:

1. What was Christopher Columbus's strange idea of the world?
2. Tell me about the adventure he had with Pirates as a young man.

Christopher Columbus, *Part 2*

It was the beginning of the time of exploration, discovery and trade! Men were questioning old ideas and wanting to find out truths for themselves. It was the perfect opportunity for a country to get rich by trading for precious, hard to find items such as spices and silks. Soon there would be a race among different European countries to claim these newly discovered places as their own.

However, there were still lots of people who held onto traditions and old fashioned ideas. Christopher Columbus had a courageous plan: if he sailed west, and the world was round, then he could reach the east. The world was just like an orange. It does not matter which way you move around the orange, you can still get to the other side. In the east were the countries of India and China, which held spices, gold and other treasures. These goods were just waiting to be found and traded for lots of money! It would make him and Portugal rich, if only someone would pay for him to try it. He approached the King of Portugal and told him of his daring plan.

"Go all the way across the ocean? It's too big, too unknown, and too dangerous! Your idea would never work!" The King of Portugal would not help.

Would Christopher give up? He could never accomplish his dream unless he found someone willing to buy him a ship, pay for sailors and all the things he would need. He decided to try another King in a different country.

In the neighboring country of Spain, there ruled both a King and a Queen. King Ferdinand and Queen Isabella were intrigued by Christopher Columbus, and once they had enough money in their treasury, they agreed to send him across the ocean in search of India and China. They sent along goods to trade and a letter for the Emperor of China himself. They expected that Christopher and his shipmates would carry back boats full of rare eastern treasures.

In August of 1492, Christopher Columbus set off to sea with three ships, the Nina, the Pinta and the Santa Maria.

Years and years had passed since Christopher had first dreamed of sailing west across the ocean. People along the way had told him it would be impossible again and again. Yet, a courageous and firm belief held him on his course. Finally, the day was here for him to prove that something entirely unheard of was also entirely possible!

Review Questions:

1. Who were the King and Queen who agreed to fund (pay for) Christopher Columbus's trip?
2. What were the names of the three ships they sailed on their voyage?

Adventures in America Week 3

	Day 1	Day 2	Day 3
Reading	Read *Christopher Columbus, Part 3*	Read *Ponce de Leon*	Read *Smart About* pg.37
Coloring/ Activity	Coloring Page, pg. 11	"Map of the World" activity	Color New Jersey on the blank US map, pg. 2
Notebook	Narration from Read Aloud, history or reader, pg. 12	Copywork, pg. 13	Fill out notebook page for New Jersey, pg. 14

Optional Read-Aloud:

Pocahontas and the Strangers

- Day 1: Chapter 11
- Day 2: Chapter 12
- Day 3: Chapter 13
- Day 4: Chapter 14
- Day 5: Chapter 15

Related Picture Books:

- *Exploration and Conquest: The Americas After Columbus: 1500-1620* by Betsy & Giulio Maestro

Possible Reader:

- *The True Story of Pocahontas*, Penner

Activity: Map of the World

Materials:
- Large brown paper bag
- Black marker
- Scissors, pencil
- Green, brown and blue water-color paints

•Cut a large rectangle from the side of the paper bag with no seam. (If you want to give your map a more antique feel, you can carefully tear the edges).

•Use a pencil to draw simple drawings of land on the left (Americas) and land on the right (Spain/ Europe).

•Paint the Americas in brown watercolor and Europe in green. Leaving some space around the edges of the land, paint the water blue.

•Once dry, use black marker to outline around the land.

•Write "New World" on the left side and "Spain" on the right. (May want to use fancy, calligraphy writing.) Draw a dotted line to make a path across the water, showing where Columbus sailed.

Optional Copywork: Ponce de Leon named the land Florida.

Notes

Christopher Columbus, Part 3

Food began to run out aboard the Nina, the Pinta and the Santa Maria, and the sailors' spirits went down along with it. Every morning they woke up to see more ocean ahead of them. All day they looked out and saw still more ocean ahead of them. And before the sun dipped down into the water on the horizon, the last thing its rays shone upon was yet more ocean ahead of them. Blue, blue and more blue.

Days went by, followed by weeks and more weeks. Men were anxiously asking each other whether Christopher Columbus could be wrong. Maybe there was no more land to the west of Spain. Maybe the ocean was so big that their food would disappear before they had a chance to look for more. The men thought longingly of the homes they had left behind. Maybe it would be better if they turned back…

What should Christopher Columbus do? Was he worried that India and China could not be reached by going west after all? The ocean was much bigger than he and others had thought. Maps and charts had been made, but they were all just guesses and the truth was that nobody really knew what was out in all that water.

Throughout all of the complaints of his men, Christopher Columbus held firmly to his plan and refused to give into their pleas to turn the ships around.

Then, one day two months after setting sail, they actually saw it right in front of them: a land of warm sunshine, sandy beaches, tropical flowers and fruits. After going ashore, they saw that there were lots of men, women and children in this place, but they did not look like what they had expected. Without even knowing it was there waiting to be discovered, Christopher Columbus had found an entire continent across the Atlantic Ocean! Of course, this was what we call North America. However, he thought he had reached India and all of its treasures!

Upon their return to Spain, the sailors were gratefully welcomed home by King Ferdinand and Queen Isabella. Everyone was very happy that the land had been claimed for trade with Spain, and more ships were sent out. Christopher Columbus journeyed to and from the new continent four times before he died.

Did he ever realize that this land was not India at all, but that it was actually a brand new discovery? We don't know that he ever knew this, but he remains famous to this day. The courage and determination that it took to pursue his dream would inspire many men to follow in his footsteps. There remained much more to be found, and others would bravely venture forth to discover it.

Review Questions:

1. How did the men feel during their voyage?
2. What was the land they finally reached? Was it what they expected?

Ponce de Leon

A man stood on the deck of a tall ship and looked out over the clear, blue-green water. Ripples moved on the surface, and the shining sunlight looked like diamonds sprinkling on the waves. They were approaching the beautiful islands of the West Indies. His name was Juan Ponce de Leon, and he was thrilled to be traveling west on Christopher Columbus's second voyage across the Atlantic Ocean. There were many, many ships with them this time. Since Columbus's first journey had proven so successful, King Ferdinand had rushed to send fleets back with more than a thousand men.

Ponce de Leon loved to sail, and he was eager to find out more about these little explored new lands. One day, several years after his first journey with Columbus, he decided to sail farther North along the coasts of the islands. Legend says that he was fervently searching to find a mysterious Fountain of Youth, which flowed with life-giving water that could heal sickness or reverse aging. Some say that Ponce de Leon wanted to postpone old age by drinking this miraculous water. It was said that anyone who drank of it would feel and look younger than they really were. However, many historians believe he was simply hunting for gold and wanting to expand the Spanish empire.

Whatever his motivation or reason was, Ponce de Leon was determined to sail. Although the currents pushed water against his ships and slowed him down, he continued farther north. He was not always sure where he was since there were no good maps to rely upon, but he kept going. At last he reached some small islands, called keys, which eventually led him to a large peninsula. There was indeed some beautifully pure and clear water here. Maybe they believed they had found a Fountain of Youth! Either way, the men were very thirsty for fresh water after only drinking from the barrels of stored water on the ships for so long. Ponce de Leon and his men probably drank eagerly and deeply from the streams they found.

Looking around them, the men saw that there were beautiful plants they had never seen before in Spain. Lush, green palm trees and bushes with large, thick foliage grew everywhere. Flowers of many different sizes and colors bloomed all around. They were absolutely beautiful! Ponce de Leon thought the land looked like a paradise. He named this green and flowering land "La Florida" which means flowers. Today we know it as the state of Florida!

Review Questions:

1. What does legend say that Ponce de Leon was searching for?
2. What is the state that Ponce de Leon found and named?

Adventures in America Week 4

	Day 1	**Day 2**	**Day 3**
Reading	Read *Amerigo Vespucci*	Read *Lost Colony of Roanoke*	Read *Smart About* pg.17 and 14
Coloring/ Activity	Coloring Page, pg. 15	"Constellation" activity	Color Georgia and Connecticut on blank US map, pg. 2
Notebook	Narration from Read Aloud, history or reader, pg. 16	Copywork, pg. 17	Fill out notebook page for Georgia and Connecticut, pgs. 18, 19

Optional Read-Aloud:

Pocahontas and the Strangers

- Day 1: Chapter 16
- Day 2: Chapter 17
- Day 3: Chapter 18
- Day 4: Chapter 19
- Day 5: Chapter 20

Related Picture Books:

- *Exploration and Conquest: The Americas After Columbus: 1500-1620* by Betsy & Giulio Maestro *(same as Week 3)*

Possible Reader:

- *The True Story of Pocahontas,* Penner

Activity: Constellation

Materials:
- Black paper
- Flashlight
- Scissors, Pencil
- White crayon
- Toothpick, nail or thumbtack

• This activity goes along with Amerigo Vespucci's love for star gazing. On one side of the black paper, have your student use the white crayon to lightly draw a picture (can be an animal or other design).

• Place a towel under the paper or set it on some carpet. Let your student use the toothpick, nail or thumbtack to make holes along the picture they drew. Varying the size and making some holes slightly bigger will make a nice picture.

• Once finished, take the picture into a dark room and hold a flashlight behind it. Turn the light on and watch the constellation shine!

Optional Copywork: We may never know for sure what happened to the Lost Colony of Roanoke.

Notes

Amerigo Vespucci

Amerigo Vespucci was born in a large, beautiful home in Florence, Italy. His parents were very rich and from the time he was a small boy, Amerigo had all of the best things. In his house were beautifully made toys, delicious foods for every meal, and servants who hurried to meet his needs. He had a private tutor who taught him many interesting subjects. Amerigo's favorite topic to learn about was the stars. He would spend his evenings gazing out his bedroom window at the sparkling sky above. There were hardly any lights coming from the city back then, and so on a cloudless night the black sky looked like it was studded with diamonds. He would find the brightest ones that he knew by name, and then trace out the pictures they formed with nearby stars. These pictures, or constellations, told stories that he loved to remember. The stars also formed a gigantic map that stretched across the whole sky. Amerigo thought of boats sailing on the seas, with only the stars to guide them to where they were going and back home again. Almost as much as he loved stars, Amerigo also loved maps. These he collected until he had quite a treasury full. He would carefully take one out at a time, open the scroll and trace the shapes of land that were drawn there. He would move his finger across the ocean, imagining that he was actually sailing a ship over those uncharted areas.

As Amerigo grew up, he became fascinated with sailing. He dreamed of sailing a ship to new places and making important discoveries, just like the famous Christopher Columbus. Columbus sailed to the west in search of Asia and returned, telling everyone how he had found India and about the peculiar Indians living there. Amerigo Vespucci became anxious to go himself. King Ferdinand, who had so generously paid for Columbus' voyages, also offered to help Amerigo Vespucci make the journey. On a ship bearing the Spanish flag, Vespucci set out west.

We don't know for sure how many voyages Vespucci made, but it might have been four. On what was probably his second trip, he began to write descriptive letters back to friends and people in Portugal and Italy. The most surprising thing that he wrote was that he didn't believe he had reached India at all! He concluded that the mass of land where his ships had landed was so huge and so entirely unknown that it must instead be a whole new continent!

A "New World" was the phrase Vespucci used in his letters. Those words got everyone's attention and before long all kinds of people were eagerly waiting to read any new letters from Vespucci. If that was indeed a new world that Columbus and Vespucci had found, the possibilities were endless! There would be new lands for explorers to discover and map. Who could imagine how much gold may be lying in the riverbeds or just underground? It was certainly exciting, and the country that first settled the land would probably become very wealthy. Vespucci's letters describing the riches of the land and the interesting customs of the native people made many Europeans interested in going to see it for themselves.

A famous map maker began drawing out maps of the new continent. It still had not been named, and it couldn't just be called the "New World" forever. The map maker decided to write Amerigo on the continents, since he was the one who had first realized it was not Asia. The maps were sent out and looked at by people far and wide. Soon, everyone was calling the new land "Amerigo." Eventually, the name was changed into "America," which sounded pretty similar. Amerigo Vespucci was not the first European to discover America, but his name lives on forever in fame!

Review Questions:

1. What was Amerigo Vespucci interested in as a boy?
2. Can you tell me why the New World was named America?

Lost Colony of Roanoke

Governor John White was a proud grandpa! Every grandfather is proud of having a grandchild born, but Governor John White had special reasons for feeling this way. His little baby granddaughter was the first, the very first English baby ever to be born in the Americas! His daughter Eleanor and her husband Ananias Dare had just welcomed a sweet little girl into their family. They gave her a beautiful name: Virginia.

Governor White and more than a hundred other men, women and children were all attempting to build a permanent English settlement in the New World. Others had come before them, but so far no one had been able to stay and actually live in America. This group hoped that they would be the ones to change that! After building some houses and a tall fence around their village, Governor White had to leave and go back to England. He kissed baby Virginia goodbye and told his daughter that he would be back soon.

It was a terrible time to sail. Weather made it difficult and dangerous, but he finally arrived in England. It proved even more difficult to get back; all the ships in England were being used to fight a war. It took a long time before Governor White found a vessel willing to carry him to Roanoke. Every day he stood alert looking out for land, eager to see his family members. Finally, they reached Roanoke on the day of little Virginia's third birthday. However, he was not prepared for the sight that greeted his eyes.

Where was everyone? What happened to all of the houses? The fence still stood sturdy as ever, but the buildings had been taken apart and moved. Every person and all of their belongings were missing and the only clue given was a word roughly carved onto a post, "Croatoan." The Croatoan were some friendly Native Americans that had lived nearby.

Although the Governor and many others searched for a long time, they never discovered exactly where the settlers went. Some historians think that they moved in with the Croatoans or other Indians, but it remains a mystery to this day. We may never know for sure what happened to the Lost Colony of Roanoke.

Review Questions:

1. Who was the first English baby born in America?
2. What did Governor John White see when he returned to Roanoke?

Adventures in America Week 5

	Day 1	Day 2	Day 3
Reading	Read *Pocahontas, Part 1*	Read *Pocahontas, Part 2*	Read *Smart About* pg.28
Coloring/ Activity	Coloring Page, pg. 21	"Headdress" activity	Color Massachusetts on blank US map, pg. 2
Notebook	Narration from Read Aloud, history or reader, pg. 22	Copywork, pg. 23	Fill out notebook page for Massachusetts, pg. 24

Optional Read-Aloud:

Pocahontas and the Strangers

- Day 1: Chapter 21
- Day 2: Chapter 22
- Day 3: Chapter 23
- Day 4: Chapter 24
- Day 5: Chapter 25

Related Picture Books:

- *Pocahontas* by Ingri & Edgar Parin D'Aulaire

Possible Reader:

- *Finding Providence*, Avi

Activity: Make a Headdress

Materials:
- Colored cardstock
- Craft feathers
- Tape/glue
- Construction paper
- Scissors

• Cut 2 two inch bands from the cardstock. Tape or staple together at one end. Estimate width of child's head and cut off excess.

• Cut out triangles from a different color of construction paper and glue onto band.

• Tape or glue feathers onto the back of the band.

• Fit around student's head and secure with tape or staples.

*Optional: You can also use glitter or sequins to decorate the band.

Optional Copywork: Pocahontas had saved their lives yet again.

Notes

Pocahontas, Part 1

In the forests of Virginia lived the playful, ten year old Pocahontas. Her father was chief of the Powhatan tribes and a very powerful man among the Indians. He was delighted with his daughter, and gave her the nickname of Pocahontas, which meant playful. She also had a secret name that was found out later, but their tribe thought that to reveal your secret name might bring you harm and so they used nicknames instead.

Pocahontas was proud of her father. He was tall and brave and had a very kingly look. Others were afraid of him, but she knew that he loved her. One day as she was helping to gather herbs near the village, she noticed a commotion nearby. Someone was yelling loudly and footsteps were hurrying towards her father's house. She cautiously followed and stood nearby the home, which was made of young saplings bent over to form a rounded frame and covered with woven reed mats. As she waited, frightened voices spoke all at once.

"Palefaces! Just like the tales told by our neighbors."

"They are here now, with magic sticks that spit out fire and make noise like thunder!"

"They have come to attack us!" an older man said anxiously.

"They will want our corn!" the man beside him moaned.

The fearful exclamations poured forth and the air felt thick with worry. They had heard stories of these palefaces, or white men, arriving in gigantic ships that the ocean waves delivered onto their shores. In many places, Indians had been kidnapped or harmed, and their seeds and food had been stolen. Were these horrifying stories about to happen to them?

Pocahontas wondered what all of this would mean. Surely these palefaces, whoever they were, would tremble in fear at the powerful Chief Powhatan. She decided there was no reason to be afraid.

Soon Pocahontas realized that her village expected that there could only be trouble between themselves and the newcomers. A handsome young captain was captured from his people. John Smith looked so different from any man Pocahontas had ever seen in her own village. His skin was pale and he seemed to wear strange skins covering his whole body. From the moment Pocahontas first saw his unusual blue eyes, she felt sure that this man was someone important. His face was full of kindness and peace, and he did not seem afraid. He was marched to the middle of the village, where the medicine men pronounced that he was dangerous and should be killed.

Review Questions:

1. Who was Pocahontas's father?
2. Why were the Indians afraid to hear that white men were nearby?

Pocahontas, Part 2

Pocahontas was shocked to hear that Captain John Smith was ordered to be killed! Immediately, she was filled with sympathy for this helpless, strange man. She ran to where he stood in the center of the wigwam.

"Please spare his life! Do not harm him!" Pocahontas cried, as she hugged his head to protect him. It was a custom among their people that a woman may ask for a prisoner to be given to her instead of executed. Although Pocahontas was far from being a woman, she felt sure that her father would not deny her wish. Chief Powhatan agreed to his daughter's request and proclaimed that John Smith would be allowed to live.

After that eventful day, Pocahontas and the white captain became good friends. She explained to him all about the tribe's way of life and John Smith described the wonders of England. The more she listened to his stories, the more Pocahontas was curious to know more about these strange men from a far away land. He told her that his men were so intent on digging for gold in this land that almost no work had been done to grow crops and prepare for winter. Eventually, John Smith was allowed to return to Jamestown, his settlement. Pocahontas was sad to see him leave.

That was not the only time Pocahontas worked to save the Englishmen's lives. Throughout the winter, the men at Jamestown were cold and grew sick. Since they had not planted crops, there was not enough food to eat and they were all fearful of starving. Pocahontas showed friendship by bringing big baskets full of corn for the men to eat. This corn helped them to survive the winter. Even after her father stopped trading with the white men, she continued to visit them, bringing along what goods she could.

Yet another time, John Smith and some friends were visiting overnight near Powhatan's village. Pocahontas overheard her father ordering an attack on the Englishmen during the night! She had to warn her friend. That evening, she snuck from the village and went to where the men were staying. She informed them of the plot against their lives. That night, John Smith's men never put down their guns. When Powhatan's warriors crept up to the house and peered inside, they found the white men armed and ready for an attack. Quickly, they abandoned their plan and ran away. Pocahontas had saved their lives again.

John Smith returned to England and Pocahontas grew up. But her connection to the white men was far from over. She married an Englishman named John Rolfe, who took her to England with him. In England, John Smith told everyone how she had saved his life and kept his men from starving. The people were impressed by the brave Indian Princess who had proven to be such a true friend to the white men!

Review Questions:

1. What are some ways Pocahontas helped the Englishmen survive?
2. What happened to Pocahontas when she grew up?

Adventures in America Week 6

	Day 1	Day 2	Day 3
Reading	Read *Journey on the Mayflower, Part 1*	Read *Journey on the Mayflower, Part 2*	Read *Smart About* pg.27 and 47
Coloring/ Activity	Coloring Page, pg. 25	"Mayflower Ship" activity	Color Maryland and South Carolina on blank US map, pg. 2
Notebook	Narration from Read Aloud, history or reader, pg. 26	Copywork, pg. 27	Fill out notebook page for Maryland and South Carolina, pgs. 28, 29

Optional Read-Aloud:

Pocahontas and the Strangers
- Day 1: Chapter 26

Squanto, Friend of the Pilgrims
- Day 2: Chapter 1
- Day 3: Chapter 2
- Day 4: Chapter 3
- Day 5: Chapter 4

Related Picture Books:
- *If You Sailed on the Mayflower in 1620* by Ann McGovern

Possible Reader:
- *Finding Providence*, Avi

Activity: Mayflower Ship

Materials:
- Egg carton
- 2 Toothpicks
- Glue and scissors
- White paper
- Clay, play dough or styrofoam

- Wash and clean the egg carton.

- Cut out one of the egg holders (for the ship).

- Push some clay, play dough or styrofoam into the bottom of the ship.

- Cut 4 small squares from the white paper (for the sails).

- Glue two squares of white paper back to back on each of the toothpicks by sandwiching the toothpick between the two pieces of white paper.

- Stick the toothpicks into the clay, play dough or styrofoam at the bottom of the egg holder.

*Optional: Your student can decorate the sails if they wish.

Optional Copywork: The Pilgrims sailed around the Cape and landed near a large rock.

Notes

Journey on the Mayflower, Part 1

Six year old Wrestling Brewster could not believe his eyes when he saw the ship's masts looming tall above him. The white sails looked clean and crisp in front of the sparkling blue ocean. The sky stretched in front of him until it finally touched the water far away. It seemed like a dream come true that they would finally be sailing away from England and journeying to the New World. Wrestling's father had told their family that they would have a new opportunity in the new world, a chance to keep their English traditions but also be free from the strict laws about religion. In England, they were not allowed to worship God the way they desired, but in the new world, there would be freedom! This group of men, women and children called themselves Pilgrims.

The Pilgrims climbed aboard the wooden ship with the pretty name, "The Mayflower," and looked around. On the deck sailors were busily preparing the ship, so the passengers went below to get out of their way. As they climbed down the ladder, the first thing everyone noticed was how low the space was. The taller men had to bend over whenever they were standing. Wrestling's family found the space that would be theirs for the voyage. His parents would sleep on a blanket laid down right on the hard wooden floor, and Wrestling and his ten year old brother, Love, would sleep on top of the trunks they had brought. Inside the two trunks were some tools they would need in the new land, some extra clothes and blankets, and an iron pot to use for cooking once they arrived. His mother hung a blanket between their space and the family's next to them. They were all so close together that they would hear every noise anyone made in the night. There were lots of children on the ship, and Wrestling looked forward to playing with the others. He had not been allowed to bring a toy with him because every last bit of space was needed for necessary items, but maybe one of the other children had brought something to play with.

A feeling of excitement and curiosity filled the Pilgrims' hearts as they felt the ship lurch and begin to move. What would the new world hold? They all knew there would be many dangers to face: bad weather at sea, not enough food, Indians that may or may not welcome them. But no matter what lay ahead, they would keep going and going, trusting God all the way. They were full of faith and courage and were completely committed to the task before them: building a new home, new community and a whole new way of life for themselves, their children, and the generations to follow. Wrestling felt proud of his parents for daring to leave familiar life behind them. He was sure that they would have a wonderful adventure.

Review Questions:

1. Why did the Pilgrims want to leave England?
2. What was the Mayflower like?

Journey on the Mayflower, Part 2

Roll, roll, roll went Wrestling's stomach, in sync with the ship's constant rolling and swaying. They had been on board for two months and by now it felt like the whole world was made of water. Wrestling didn't think he could eat anything anymore; he was so tired of the hard biscuits and moldy cheese. Even those unappetizing foods were beginning to run out and he could tell everyone was worried. Would the food last for the entire voyage? How would they have any strength to build a settlement once they arrived, if they were all weakened by hunger? At least the terrible waves had lessened by now and the pounding rain had stopped. That powerful storm had had them all terrified as the ship had been tossed up and down and side to side. Calm blue water surrounded them now, but the air was getting colder and there was still no land in sight.

"Land Ho!" Came a cry as someone jumped up and down on the deck. Everyone crowded at the railing to strain their eyes. At first, it just looked like water as far as they could see; then something fuzzy and small appeared on the horizon. Could it be? Yes! As they moved on it became larger and they could tell it was indeed land. Sandy hills dotted the landscape as the Pilgrims approached the beaches of Cape Cod.

They were much farther north than they had meant to be. They had wanted to be closer to Jamestown, the settlement begun by Captain John Smith. The storm must have moved them off their course. Farther north meant colder weather, and it meant that they were nowhere near Jamestown, where there were others who could help them begin their own settlement. Cape Cod is a long, sandy piece of land that sticks out of the state of Massachusetts. They sailed around the cape and landed near a large rock. The rock was a perfect place to come onto land. They had sailed from Plymouth, England and so they named this new place Plymouth. That rock is called Plymouth Rock today.

Wrestling and Love were thrilled to stand on solid ground that didn't roll under their feet. They were so happy that they and several others fell to their knees and thanked God. After two months of near starvation, storms and uncertainty, the Pilgrims had finally reached the New World! They looked at each other, barely containing their excitement. Surely everything would be alright now. They just had to build some houses before snow fell. There must be food nearby to make them all strong again. The boys looked around at the sandy ground and the trees below a bright blue sky. This was their new home.

Review Questions:

1. What were some of the problems the Pilgrims faced during their voyage?
2. Where did the Mayflower land?

Adventures in America Week 7

	Day 1	**Day 2**	**Day 3**
Reading	Read *Plymouth Plantation*	Read *Squanto*	Read *Smart About* pg.36
Coloring/ Activity	Coloring Page, pg. 31	"(Pop) Corn Cobs" activity	Color New Hampshire on blank US map, pg. 2
Notebook	Narration from Read Aloud, history or reader, pg. 32	Copywork, pg. 33	Fill out notebook page for New Hampshire, pg. 34

Optional Read-Aloud:

Squanto, Friend of the Pilgrims
- Day 1: Chapter 5
- Day 2: Chapter 6
- Day 3: Chapter 7
- Day 4: Chapter 8
- Day 5: Chapter 9

Related Picture Books:

- *The Thanksgiving Story* by Dalgliesh

Possible Reader:

- *Sam the Minute Man*, Benchley

Activity: (Pop) Corn Cobs

Materials:
- Popcorn   -Scissors
- Craft glue
- Yellow and green construction paper

• Cut 2 large corn cob shapes from yellow paper.

• Cut 4 husk shapes from the green paper, slightly larger than the corn cobs.

• Glue the husks behind the corn cobs, fanning out slightly.

• Spread glue over the front of the corn cob and stick on pop-corn.

Optional Copywork: With Squanto's help, the Pilgrims were able to plant all the corn they would need for the winter.

Notes

Plymouth Plantation

Constance Hopkins steeped the fresh herbs in water that her mother had boiled in a large iron pot over the fire. She felt terrible for all the sick people who were shivering under thin blankets in one of the houses the men had managed to build before the snow deepened. She carried the hot tea into the sick room and looked at the beds crowded together. Raspy coughs could be heard from outside the walls, and inside the sound was awful. The smell was pretty bad, too, since there was no way to wash the soiled bedding and clothes as often as was needed. Constance gave a kind smile to the various invalids as she offered them hot tea. Many cheered up enough to smile back and chat about what the others were doing outside.

The men had hurried to build several houses that lined the one road that ran through the village. They gave the road a simple name: the Street. For now, families had to share the houses. Once the winter snows melted, they would be able to build enough homes for everyone. The winter was cold and harsh. They had never experienced such cold back in England. Without enough food, the Pilgrims were not strong enough to fight off sickness. One by one, they became sick and died. Many wondered if any of them would even survive the winter. Constance was thankful that both of her parents and her three brothers and sisters had stayed healthy. Even tiny Oceanus, who had been born during the voyage over the ocean, was growing strong.

When it seemed doubtful that the Pilgrims could survive any longer on their meager food supplies, help came in an unexpected form. One day, a tall Indian man walked right into Plymouth. He walked boldly up the Street that ran through the village and looked as if he might walk right into the common house. Some men quickly approached him and made it clear that he was welcome among them, since the Pilgrims wanted and needed to be at peace with their neighbors. They wondered how they would ever communicate, when the Indian finally opened his mouth and spoke.

"Hello, Englishmen!"

He spoke English! The man's name was Samoset, and Constance thought he looked quite strange at first with his bronze skin and long hair. He stood taller than any of the Pilgrim men, and his face was brave and proud looking. He held a bow and two arrows, and the bow was almost as long as a man! He looked fearless and strong, and the Pilgrims immediately showed him respect.

Review Questions:

1. What were some problems the Pilgrims faced during their first winter?
2. Who was the first Indian that made friends with the Pilgrims?

Squanto

Samoset, the English speaking Indian who had introduced himself to the Pilgrims that winter day, also introduced another helpful friend. Squanto spoke even better English than Samoset, and he was able to offer the Pilgrims the help they would need to survive the winter.

The Pilgrims had heard through stories told by other explorers that thousands of Indians lived along the East coast of America. They were rather surprised once they arrived and could hardly find any! Although there were empty wigwams here and there, there was no sign of Indian tribes living in the area.

Squanto answered their questions about this. White men who had come on other ships before the Pilgrims had brought something terrible along with them without even knowing it. They carried strange new germs, new diseases that the Indians had never faced before. Their bodies were not prepared to fight these illnesses, and they became sick. More and more died and even whole villages were wiped out by sickness. The fields the Indians had prepared for growing corn still remained, but the hardworking people who had made them were all gone.

Squanto offered to help the Pilgrims plant corn and other vegetables around their plantation. He even taught them a trick for making the corn grow! He made a small hill of soil, mixed in the corn seed, and placed some small dead fish, called Alewives, in with the dirt and seeds. The rotting fish fertilized the earth and helped the corn grow big and healthy. The Pilgrims had brought along many kinds of seeds from England. These English seeds grew poorly in the foreign soil. If they had not had the "Indian" crops, there would never have been enough food for them all. With Squanto's help, the Pilgrims were able to plant all the corn they would need for the next winter, along with squash, beans, pumpkins and other native crops.

Squanto had another very important job in helping the Pilgrims. He could speak his tribe's language, and he could also speak English. This enabled him to be a translator between the Indians and the Englishmen. He would listen to what one side had to say, and then put that into words the other side could understand. Without understanding each other, it would have been impossible to become friends. It was very important to the Pilgrims that the Indians become their friends instead of being enemies. It would not have been possible for that to happen without Squanto's words to help!

Review Questions:

1. What had happened to the Indians who used to live in the land?
2. In what ways did Squanto help the Pilgrims?

Adventures in America Week 8

	Day 1	Day 2	Day 3
Reading	Read *Working to Survive*	Read *Thanksgiving*	Read *Smart About* pg.53 and 39
Coloring/ Activity	Coloring Page, pg. 35	"Cow Cumbers" activity	Color Virginia and New York on blank US map, pg. 2
Notebook	Narration from Read Aloud, history or reader, pg. 36	Copywork, pg. 37	Fill out notebook page for Virginia and New York, pgs. 38, 39

Optional Read-Aloud:

Squanto, Friend of the Pilgrims
- Day 1: Chapter 10
- Day 2: Chapter 11
- Day 3: Chapter 12
- Day 4: Chapter 13
- Day 5: Chapter 14

Related Picture Books:

- *If You Were at the First Thanksgiving* by Anne Kamma

Possible Reader:

- *Sam the Minute Man*, Benchley

Activity: Cow Cumbers

Materials:
- 1/2 cup distilled white vinegar
- 2 tsp. salt
- 1 cup white sugar
- 3 cups sliced cucumbers
- 1 cup sliced onions

• Bring vinegar, salt and sugar to a boil on the stove. Boil until the sugar has completely dissolved.

• Place sliced cucumbers and onions in a large bowl and pour the hot vinegar mixture over them. Put into jars or other sterile containers and store in the refrigerator.

** This is different than how the Pilgrims would have made pickles. I chose this recipe for the sake of both convenience and taste. If you would like a more authentic method, simply research online and you will find several options.

Optional Copywork: With homes and storehouses filled with food, the Pilgrims decided to have a feast.

Notes

Working to Survive

Once spring arrived, half of the Pilgrims had died from sickness, hunger and cold. The Mayflower prepared to sail back to England, and the captain asked if any Pilgrims wanted to return with him on the ship. They had faced terrible struggles and lost friends and family members. Should they give up and go back? No, not one single Pilgrim was aboard the Mayflower during the return journey! They all stayed committed to the idea that God had led them so far and that He would help them create a new life in the new world.

Throughout the spring, Squanto helped the Pilgrims plant crops. The men built more buildings through the summer and the women worked at gardens and preserved foods. Even the children were very busy! Boys and girls helped collect the little fishes to mix in with the corn seed. They dug up mussels, clams and eels to eat. They helped weed the gardens, wash the laundry and knead bread dough. There was always plenty of work to be done!

Damaris Hopkins' least favorite jobs were making soap and roasting meat. Wash day was dreaded by most of the children. First, they had to make the soap from ashes and animal fat, and it smelled pretty awful! Then Damaris and other kids helped carry water in heavy buckets from the river. This had to be boiled in huge kettles. After the dirty clothes and bedding had been scrubbed thoroughly, the children would twist the dripping water off them, before spreading them out to dry on bushes and trees. It wasn't too bad if the sun was shining and the air was warm, but on cold days her hands ached from holding the icy wet clothes. Roasting the meat was another tedious job, because it meant sitting by the smoky fire for hours and turning the spit continuously. The meat was sliced and skewered onto long iron "spits" and then placed over an open fire to cook. Damaris preferred kneading the bread dough, or even pounding grain into flour instead of sitting by the hot fire. However, complaining was never allowed. In order to survive, everybody had to be willing to work happily. She knew everyone felt the burden of the hard work, but a desire to make it through the winter drove them on.

Once the plants and vegetables had grown nice and big, the Pilgrims harvested their crops. They put corn into baskets and hung up sliced vegetables to dry. They even salted meat so that it would last during the cold winter months when hunting would be impossible. Some vegetables were pickled so they would not spoil. "Cow cumbers" (pickled cucumbers) were a delicious treat that the children especially enjoyed.

With homes and storehouses filled with food, the Pilgrims decided to have a feast. Some men hunted wild turkeys and the women prepared corn, pumpkin, beans and dried fruits. Everyone looked forward to taking several days off from work to eat and celebrate. Surely this next winter would be better than the last!

Review Questions:

1. What were some of the jobs of the children?
2. How did the Pilgrims store food?

Thanksgiving

Early in the morning Damaris awoke to the noise of the rooster crowing. Every day except Sunday, her family arose before the sun was up in order to accomplish as much work as could be done before darkness fell in the evening. Today would be different. Although there was still food for the women and children to prepare, it would also be a day of games and celebration. Today the Pilgrims would begin their first Harvest Festival in the new world.

Damaris and her brothers and sister slept crowded together on a trundle bed. It was actually just a mattress in a drawer that could be pushed back under their parents' bed during the day. The small house was too crowded for much furniture. There was one room, called the hall. At mealtimes, their parents sat on barrels and used a board for a table. The children ate their meals standing up. Today they would set up some boards on top of barrels to use for tables outside in the Street, since no one had had any time to build fancy new furniture yet.

Damaris put on her dress over her shift and fixed her hair tightly into her coif, which was a small cap that sat on top of her head. She laced her boots and helped her mother dress baby Oceanus. Her brother and sister were talking about who would win the footraces that day. As she listened to their excited chatter, Damaris' heart beat faster just imagining how much fun they were about to have. Ever since they had boarded the Mayflower, there had been too much work to do just to survive that no one had given a thought to playing games. Even the children rarely took a break to play. This would be a special treat for everyone! Soon the whole family was ready for the festivities.

Her father had left with some other men yesterday and had hunted many wild turkeys, geese and ducks. The women had busily ground flour from grain to bake into bread. Today they would work together to stew eels, roast ducks and bake cornbread. After the scanty rations on the ship and during the winter, everyone was eagerly looking forward to a plentiful feast.

Suddenly, anxious whispers could be heard outside their house. She walked out the door to see a huge group of about one hundred Indians coming into the village! There were even more Indians than Pilgrims! How would they ever feed so many people? Her heart sank some as she thought that maybe it wouldn't be quite a feast after all.

"Hark! They have brought five deer!" Her father's voice sounded relieved.

Indeed they had. Five men each carried a deer slung across his shoulders. Deer meat was an extra special treat for the Pilgrims, something they had been too poor to eat in England. There was more than enough food for everyone!

There was so much to celebrate at that first Harvest Festival, which we now call Thanksgiving. The long, hard year was over. They had survived, and even though there was heartache from all their losses, there was a strong hope that their future would be a good one. They were people who would not give up.

Review Questions:

1. What were the Pilgrims' houses like?
2. Why did the Pilgrims want to celebrate?

Adventures in America Week 9

	Day 1	Day 2	Day 3
Reading	Read *William Penn*	Read *Daniel Boone*	Read *Smart About* pg.40
Coloring/ Activity	Coloring Page, pg. 41	"Follow the Tracks" activity	Color North Carolina on blank US map, pg. 2
Notebook	Narration from Read Aloud, history or reader, pg. 42	Copywork, pg. 43	Fill out notebook page for North Carolina, pg. 44

Optional Read-Aloud:

A Lion to Guard Us
- Day 1: Chapter 1
- Day 2: Chapter 2
- Day 3: Chapter 3
- Day 4: Chapter 4
- Day 5: Chapter 5

Related Picture Books:

- *Daniel Boone: Woodsman of Kentucky* by John Paul Zronik

Possible Reader:

- *George the Drummer Boy*, Benchley

Activity: Follow the Tracks

Materials:
-Dried beans   -Small stones or bits of torn tissue
-Toy animals (plastic or stuffed)

•Tell your student that they are about to act like Daniel Boone and track down some different wild animals (show the toy animals). Assign a type of track for each animal used (dried beans for one, tissue for another, etc.). Without your student watching, hide each animal in a different room or part of the room, and then leave a track to be followed. Once your tracks have been laid, let your student follow the tracks to find the game!

*Optional: You can give your student a flashlight and have them shine light on each animal once it is found.

Optional Copywork: Daniel Boone had successfully blazed a trail into what became known as the state of Kentucky!

Notes

William Penn

Back in England, there was a young boy with a famous father, Sir Admiral William Penn. His father fought bravely in the English navy and was well respected by all. When William was just a little boy, he caught a dreadful disease called smallpox. Smallpox was a terrible problem at the time because there were still no vaccinations to prevent people from getting sick. Many times smallpox left a person completely blind, or even worse. Fortunately, William recovered fully, but not until he had already lost all of his hair. For the rest of his life, William would always wear a wig.

After his frightening sickness, William's family moved from the city to the quiet countryside. Away from the crowds and noise of the city, William could rest and grow strong. He loved the smell of the grass and seeing how plants grew. He also loved to run as fast as he could over the fields and rolling hills near his home. It was a wonderful place for a child to live!

Once William grew up, he chose to become a Quaker. A Quaker is a Christian who is a pacifist. A pacifist does not believe in fighting, violence or wars. William wrote a lot about being a Quaker, and that made some people in England angry. He was arrested several times for his strong religious beliefs. Eventually, he was given a large amount of money after his father's death, and William chose to use it buying land in America. Along with many other Quakers, he left England and bargained with the Delaware Indians to buy a large piece of land on the East Coast. He wanted to name the colony "Sylvania," which means "forests" in Latin. Then he decided to name it after his father, so it became "Pennsylvania."

Besides founding the state of Pennsylvania, William Penn made another important contribution to the country. He wrote about his ideas for a government. A government is how a group of people, like a state or a country, is run. He thought there should be something called amendments, which means that changes would be allowed to be made. That way, if someone had an idea for a change, they could do it peacefully through the law instead of fighting and using violence. William Penn's thoughts about this type of a government would be very significant in the future of America.

Review Questions:

1. Tell me about William Penn's religion.
2. What were some important things William Penn did?

Daniel Boone: Frontier Man

In Pennsylvania there also lived a brave and daring young boy named Daniel. He learned to read and write, but beyond that he had little interest in schooling. His passions were all found in the great outdoors, where he would run and explore over the fields, through the woods and following the rivers. He enjoyed the quiet of being alone in the forest with the animals for company. At twelve years old, he was given his first rifle, and he soon developed a love for hunting. It was great fun to find out the hiding places of wild animals like panthers, bears and wolves. He quickly became a master tracker and could follow an animal through the wilderness, which was normally a skill that only the Indians could do very well.

One legend about Daniel says that one day he was out hunting with some other young boys. They were excitedly following the trails of some deer and were bragging about who would have the best shot. Suddenly the calm quiet of the forest was broken by the loud scream of a panther! Panthers were greatly feared because they could attack quite brutally. The young boys were terrified and ran away as quickly as they could, stumbling over roots and fallen branches in their haste. Daniel, however, raised his rifle and waited until just when the panther was leaping towards him, then fired a shot right through the animal's heart. Daniel's friends eventually returned to see what had happened to him, and were shocked to find him with the panther slung over his shoulders. His bravery and skill had won him an impressive reputation!

Daniel Boone grew up, was married, and lived in a little log cabin in the woods. To support his family, he would go on long hunts every fall. For weeks and even months at a time he hiked through the wilderness, returning home with heaps of deerskins, beaver and otter. These were then traded for lots of money. Buckskins became known as "bucks", which is still a nickname for the American dollar today!

Daniel had heard about land on the other side of the mountains that was made of rich soil which would grow crops easily. He had also heard that there were still lots of wild animals, or "game" in those lands. The colonies were quickly becoming crowded as more and more settlers arrived and tamed the wilderness into farms and villages. He was curious about this mysterious land that was still only inhabited by Indian tribes. With a group of fellow travelers, he began to journey west and made a trail through to the other side of the Appalachian Mountains.

As they traveled, Daniel entertained his comrades around the evening campfire. Although never an eager student, Daniel had developed a love for reading. He always brought along a book or two wherever he ventured. Some of his favorites were the Holy Bible and Gulliver's Travels. Listening to Daniel read aloud and watching the flickering flames of the fire were restful treats for his men at the end of wearying days.

Once they had passed through the mountains, they set eyes upon a truly rich land. The soil would yield an abundance of crops, and the forests were teeming with deer and other animals. Daniel Boone had successfully blazed a trail into what became known as the state of Kentucky!

Review Questions:

1. What skills did Daniel Boone have?
2. What was the name of the state Daniel Boone helped to explore and settle?

Adventures in America Week 10

	Day 1	Day 2	Day 3
Reading	Read *Benjamin Franklin, Part 1*	Read *Benjamin Franklin, Part 2*	Read *Smart About* pg.46 and 52
Coloring/ Activity	Coloring Page, pg. 45	"Create Your Own Invention" activity	Color Rhode Island and Vermont on blank US map, pg. 2
Notebook	Narration from Read Aloud, history or reader, pg. 46	Copywork, pg. 47	Fill out notebook page for Rhode Island and Vermont, pgs. 48, 49

Optional Read-Aloud:

A Lion to Guard Us
- Day 1: Chapter 6
- Day 2: Chapter 7
- Day 3: Chapter 8-9
- Day 4: Chapter 10
- Day 5: Chapter 11

Related Picture Books:

- *Benjamin Franklin* by Ingri & Edgar Parin D'Aulaire

Possible Reader:

- *George the Drummer Boy*, Benchley

Activity: Create Your Own Invention

•Discuss with your student how inventions are often thought of (i.e. needing a more convenient way of doing something, from an experiment "gone wrong," etc.).

•Ask what new thing your student would like to invent. Encourage them to think creatively and have fun exploring the possibilities.

•Give them a piece of paper. Write the name of their invention at the top and let them draw a picture of the idea below. If your child is inspired to actually create their invention, consider giving them odd and ends materials (empty tissue paper rolls, masking tape, pieces of cardboard, etc.). Remember to take a picture!

Optional Copywork: Benjamin Franklin had proven that lightning and electricity were the same thing!

Notes

Benjamin Franklin, Part 1: The Secret Writer

After William Penn, there was another very important man in Pennsylvania. Although he was born in Boston, Benjamin Franklin would do many great things in the city of Philadelphia, in Pennsylvania.

Benjamin Franklin was the tenth child out of seventeen siblings! Imagine having sixteen brothers and sisters! He had a happy childhood with lots of playmates always available for games. Although it was very hard to receive a good education, he learned to read and developed a love of books. He was very curious and hardworking, so learning new things was a joy for him. His father wanted him to be a clergyman and work for a church. Clergymen needed special training, though, and his father could not afford to pay for that.

Once he was old enough, Benjamin helped his older brother in the printing business. They printed out newspapers and other materials for people to read. Once they were printed, Benjamin took them out into the streets to sell them. Benjamin desperately wanted to write, but knew that his big brother, James, would not print anything written by him. He came up with a plan. Late at night, Benjamin stayed awake and secretly wrote wonderful, witty letters for the newspaper, but he did it under a secret name! Instead of signing the letters with the name of Benjamin Franklin, he wrote "Silence Dogood" as the name of the writer. He wanted everyone to think that an old lady was writing these letters instead of him. His plan worked and people were so impressed with the letters that Silence Dogood became quite famous. After writing sixteen of those letters, Benjamin finally confessed that he himself was really the author. Just like he had expected, his brother was very angry. Benjamin had to leave and that was when he traveled to Philadelphia.

In Philadelphia, Benjamin worked as an apprentice in another print shop. After awhile, he realized that he was a better printer than the man he was working for! He opened his own printing shop. He started a newspaper and wrote a book called "Poor Richard's Almanac." An almanac was a book filled with weather reports, recipes, advice and all kinds of other information. Most families had only two or three books in their homes. One was the Holy Bible and the other was usually an almanac. Farmers consulted their almanacs so they could know when they should plant their crops. Housewives looked in the almanac for recipes and home remedies for sicknesses. This was another time when Benjamin pretended someone else was the writer! Everyone thought a poor farmer named Richard was writing the book, instead of Benjamin! Today people still quote many of the sayings that were inside. Maybe you have heard these: "A penny saved is a penny earned." "A place for everything, everything in its place." "Honesty is the best policy."

Benjamin Franklin is famous for many, many reasons. His writings helped form the country we have today. Later, as we will see, he even helped write one of the most important papers in American history!

Review Questions:

1. Tell me something about Benjamin Franklin's childhood.
2. What were some things that Benjamin Franklin wrote?

Benjamin Franklin, Part 2: Something New

Benjamin Franklin was not just a writer. He also loved science and doing experiments. He was very interested in figuring out how things worked. He was an inventor. An inventor has a new idea and creates something that can help make life easier. Benjamin Franklin had lots of new ideas and invented many things.

Winters in Philadelphia were snowy and cold. People liked to stay inside their houses, bundled up in blankets to keep warm. Every house had a stove for cooking, but the stoves did not give off much heat. To stay warm, you had to stand so close to the stove that your clothes were in danger of catching fire! Benjamin Franklin thought about this problem and came up with a solution. He invented a new kind of stove that still sent the smoke up the chimney, but let the heat stay in the house. There was even a little door in front of the fire to make it extra safe. The Franklin stove was a huge success!

Another dangerous problem in Philadelphia was house fires. Fires would often start and destroy whole buildings before they could be put out. Benjamin Franklin was concerned about fires and thought that there should be an organized group of men ready to put out a fire anywhere at any time. This became the first Fire Department! Before long every city would have their own Fire Department, and many houses and lives would be saved.

Since he was a child, Benjamin Franklin had loved books. He wanted everyone to be able to read as many books as they wanted. This was very important to him, so he started the first Public Library.

Benjamin Franklin invented other things, such as swim fins and bifocals (glasses to help eyes see things far away, and also help eyes read small print in books up close). One of his most important inventions had to do with electricity. Other scientists had begun performing experiments about electricity, and Benjamin Franklin had the idea that lightning might be the same thing. One day, he took a kite with a long string and a key at the end of it and flew it high up in a cloud where there was some lightning. A small bolt of lightning struck the kite and sent electrical current all the way down the string to the key! Benjamin Franklin had proven that lightning and electricity were the same thing! That helped him come up with another great idea for keeping houses safe from fire: the lightning rod. A lightning rod is a metal pole that sticks up from the roof of a house. During a storm, lightning hits the rod instead of hitting the roof and setting the house on fire. Benjamin Franklin was always inventing something new!

Review Questions:

1. What does an inventor do?
2. What were some of Benjamin Franklin's inventions?

Adventures in America Week 11

	Day 1	Day 2	Day 3
Reading	Read *A Colonial Farm*	Read *A Colonial Town*	Read *Smart About* pg.24 and 49
Coloring/ Activity	Coloring Page, pg. 51	"Making Butter" activity	Color Kentucky and Tennessee on blank US map, pg. 2
Notebook	Narration from Read Aloud, history or reader, pg. 52	Copywork, pg. 53	Fill out notebook page for Kentucky and Tennessee, pgs. 54, 55

Optional Read-Aloud:

A Lion to Guard Us
- Day 1: Chapter 12
- Day 2: Chapter 13-14
- Day 3: Chapter 15
- Day 4: Chapter 16-17
- Day 5: Chapter 18

Related Picture Books:
- *If You Lived in Colonial Times* by Ann McGovern

Possible Reader:
- *The 18 Penny Goose*, Walker

Optional Copywork: There was always food to be prepared, clothes to be mended and work to be done.

Activity: Making Butter

Materials:
-Heavy whipping cream (full fat), as much as you wish to make into butter   -Pinch of salt, if desired
-Clean jar with tight fitting lid   -Marble

•Let the whipping cream sit on counter until it reaches room temperature.

•You may want to show your student pictures of a butter churner from a book or the internet while you wait.

•Pour the cream into the jar, filling almost to the top. Add a marble to the jar (if you don't have one, it will not affect the process). Tightly screw on the lid.

•Shake! Shake! Shake! You may want to involve several family members and let everyone take a turn. Playing some music and dancing around would make this even more fun (although I can't say that they did that in Colonial times).

•After you have shaken it hard for about thirty minutes, add a pinch of salt and whip with a fork. It should be a nice, spreadable consistency at this point. You can shake it longer if desired.

•Eat on bread, toast, pancakes, cornbread or anything!

Notes

A Colonial Farm

By this time the King of England had decided that there were thirteen separate colonies in North America that were all under his rule. From as far as today's Maine in the North, down to Georgia in the South was all considered part of England. The colonies were called New Hampshire, Rhode Island, New York, Connecticut, Massachusetts, New Jersey, Pennsylvania, Maryland, Delaware, Virginia, North Carolina, South Carolina and Georgia. Each colony had its own self government, or way of ruling itself. Each colony was different from the others, and life was also different on the farms than it was in the towns.

Ten year old Abigail woke up to the cries of her baby brother George. George slept down in the parlor in a wooden cradle next to their parents' bed. That same wooden cradle had held Abigail, too, as well as her six other brothers and sisters. Once a child outgrew the cradle, they moved up to sleep on the loft with the rest of the children. Abigail heard the rustle of her mother's full skirts moving around the hall downstairs. She knew that she should hurry down to help feed George so her mother could finish making breakfast. Abigail slipped into her long dress and laced up her black boots before climbing down the ladder.

"Good morning to thee!" Mother greeted Abigail with a smile on her young face. She had married and had her eight children at an early age, and was still young and pretty.

"Good morning to thee, Mother." Abigail picked up baby George and held him on her lap as she sat on one of the long benches at their wooden table that Father had made himself. She offered him some bits of cooked pumpkin and made faces to coax a smile from his chubby face. Soon he had finished eating and Abigail set him on the floor to crawl around while she helped Mother churn some milk into butter to eat with their hotcakes for breakfast. As she worked the milk into thick, creamy butter, her thoughts wandered over their life on the farm.

Abigail enjoyed working in the kitchen. Her mother knew how to do so many things and Abigail's greatest wish was to learn how to do them just as well. In the years to come, Abigail would probably marry a hard working farmer herself, and then it would be her job to make soap and candles, spin wool into yarn, and knit and sew clothing for her family. Mother tried hard to train her daughters in the crafts they would one day need.

With the fire blazing cheerfully under the chimney and filling the large hall with warmth, the house felt comfortable and cozy. Like all other farming families in New Jersey, Abigail's house was made from strong wooden beams and stood one and half stories tall. Besides the hall where they worked and ate their meals, the first floor also held the parlor and her parents' bed. A ladder led upstairs to a loft where large mattresses lay next to each other on the wooden boards. From the loft's small window, the children could look out over the fields and watch them change from freshly plowed dirt in the spring into tall rows of corn in the summer. Next to the house was the garden where they all helped clear weeds between the growing vegetables and herbs. On the other side of the garden, standing sturdy and tall beside the fields, was their two story wooden barn. The boys would be in and out of the barn all day long helping Father.

There was always food to be prepared, clothes to be mended and work to be done. It was a quiet, steady sort of work, though, and life did not feel busy or rushed. Abigail felt a peaceful contentment fill her heart as she watched her mother cheerfully care for her family.

Review Questions:

1. What kinds of work did Colonial women do on a farm?
2. What was Abigail's home like?

A Colonial Town

William hopped off the road just in time before a spirited stallion pranced by. He glanced up and saw that the rider was a tall man wearing a powdered white wig and a handsomely cut gray coat. The man frowned at the young boy who had nearly been run over by his horse, then rode quickly on his way. Seven year old William felt his cheeks redden with embarrassment as he ducked into the Mercantile where he had been headed.

"Hello, there, lad. What does your mother need this day?" asked Mr. Hutchins.

"If you please, sir, she wishes to buy a pound of sugar and some molasses. Also, she asks if any more embroidery needles have arrived from England?" William replied.

"Hmmm, yes, she is in luck! The boat that harbored two days ago brought shipments." Mr. Hutchins weighed sugar on a scale and wrapped it in paper along with the molasses and two needles. After tying a string around the package, he handed it to William. William gave him the coins he had brought in his pocket and left with his mother's purchase. She was home with his five year old brother and two little sisters. His father was on a large trading vessel sailing to England to deliver stores of mackerel and cod that had been fished in the plentiful waters along the New England shores. He sailed back and forth between the continents each year, and William was used to taking care of the family during his father's absence. He looked forward to the day when he would be old enough to accompany his father on those voyages. More than anything, William longed to sail the beautiful wooden ships with the clean white sails over the blue water. He wanted to sail far away from land and be surrounded by waves as far as his eyes could see.

Born in Boston, Massachusetts, William had spent his life looking out from the shore at the busy harbors and the Atlantic Ocean spread out before him. He had heard story after story about the adventures of a life at sea. Not that the town wasn't also full of excitement in its own way. There were men like Mr. Samuel Adams who walked the streets talking loudly about freedom and self government. There were fishermen and ship builders bustling near the harbors and ship yards. The roads were lined with shops, stables, taverns and factory storefronts. There were always new people settling in and starting various businesses. Newly constructed buildings popped up every few months, and the noise on the streets got louder as time went by. It was one of the largest towns in New England.

William arrived at his large two-story home, walked through the parlor and passed the library to where his mother sat in the dining room, consulting with the kitchen maid. He set the parcel from the store down on the table and stood proudly before her. She thanked him for being such a blessing and a help to her when Father was away. William felt happy to be useful and needed here, but in his heart he longed for the day he would be a grown man at sea just like his father.

Review Questions:

1. What was the town of Boston like?
2. What kind of job did William's father have?

Adventures in America Week 12

	Day 1	**Day 2**	**Day 3**
Reading	Read *Young George Washington*	Read *George Washington Grows Up*	Read *Smart About* pg.42
Coloring/ Activity	Coloring Page, pg. 57	"Cherry Tree Painting" activity	Color Ohio on blank US map, pg. 2
Notebook	Narration from Read Aloud, history or reader, pg. 58	Copywork, pg. 59	Fill out notebook page for Ohio, pg. 60

Optional Read-Aloud:

A Lion to Guard Us
- Day 1: Chapter 19
- Day 2: Chapter 20
- Day 3: Chapter 21
- Day 4: Chapter 22
- Day 5: Chapter 23

Related Picture Books:

- *George Washington* by Ingri & Edgar Parin D'Aulaire

Possible Reader:

- *The 18 Penny Goose*, Walker

Activity: Cherry Tree Painting

Materials:
- Light blue construction paper   -Paper plate
- Brown, green and red paint   -Newspaper

•Spread newspaper on table to protect surface. Pour small amounts of brown, green and red paint onto a paper plate.

•Let your student use their fingers or paintbrushes to create a cherry tree, with a brown trunk and branches, green leaves and red thumbprints as the cherries.

•Under the tree, write "(child's name) tell the truth."

•Let dry and take a picture!

Optional Copywork: Honesty was something that George Washington valued highly.

Notes

Young George Washington

Not too long after the Pilgrims had sailed on the Mayflower and set up a colony at Plymouth, a man named John Washington arrived on another ship from England. He came to Virginia, not far from where Jamestown had been started years ago. Over time, more and more settlers arrived in Virginia, building towns and villages. John Washington went into the wilderness away from other people and cleared a large farm. This farm became the home of his son, then his grandson and eventually his great-grandson, George. Little George Washington soon moved to a different farm nearby, which was so large that it was called a plantation. There was a large, beautiful house and field after field of crops and pastures. It was a wonderful place for an energetic young boy to grow up.

George was a very smart little boy, even though he did not go to school for very long. He learned to read and soon had read many classical books from England. He learned to write well and carefully copied sentences into his copybook. Mostly he copied words about how to have nice manners and treat other people well. He was trained in geography and mathematics. He was especially interested in how to use math in measuring land and drawing maps. His mother taught him stories from the Bible, and George learned the importance of being honest and kind.

Honesty was something that George valued highly. There is a well-known story about George Washington's honesty, and although it may not be a true story, it is worth telling. George's father had orchards full of different kinds of trees. There were peach trees, apple trees and a young cherry tree. The cherry tree was one of Mr. Washington's prized possessions, and he asked everyone on the farm to take special care of it. One day, young George was given a shiny, sharp new axe. He was thrilled with his axe and eagerly left the house to try it outside. He walked through the gardens, now and then swinging his axe at a branch to test its blade. He was pleased to see how swiftly the axe chopped through the wood. Walking through the orchards, he came upon the young cherry tree. Eying the trunk carefully, George guessed that his axe would cut through its wood quite easily. He lifted the axe and with a swift, decided effort, he swung right through the bark and into the wood of the tree. He had almost cut it down! Surely just one more swing would complete the job. Again he lifted the axe and let it go, chopping through the trunk and sending the tree crashing down to the orchard floor.

As the tree hit the ground with a thud, George's heart thumped with sudden realization. He had just cut down his father's favorite tree! That afternoon, his father strolled through the grounds to check on the crops and trees. He was startled to arrive at the place where his young cherry tree had stood just yesterday. Surprised and angry, he questioned George.

"Do you know who chopped down my cherry tree?" his father asked sternly. George's face whitened as he looked his father in the eye.

"It was I, Father, I cannot tell a lie." George replied in shame.

George's father softened as he gazed at his son. Gently, he told George that he would rather have a son who was honest and always told the truth more than an orchard full of cherry trees.

Review Questions:

1. What did young George Washington do to his father's cherry tree?
2. How did George answer his father's question about what had happened to the tree?

George Washington Grows Up

Young George Washington continued to learn valuable skills as he grew up. Even without much schooling, he became an expert in using mathematics to measure and map out the land. He was eager to learn all that he could, and spent his evenings poring over books and practicing drawing maps. His days were full of a different kind of training. By working alongside his older half-brother, Lawrence, he learned about growing crops and taking care of farm animals. Soon he was very skilled in farming the land, raising livestock and surveying.

Eventually people began hiring George Washington to do the important job of surveying their land. Many large farms, called plantations, had lands that stretched far into the wilderness. The owners often did not know exactly how much land they had or what it contained. George Washington took long trips through the wilderness, measuring the land and carefully drawing maps. He wrote down all the things he observed, such as what kinds of wildlife there were, whether there were any Indians or fur traders living on the land, and where rivers, ponds and lakes were. He became very familiar with the lands throughout Virginia, and learned how to survive in the outdoors on his own.

George also loved to have fun. He became a great dancer, fisherman, hunter and horseman. In fact, he excelled at just about everything he tried. He was taller than many men, strong and muscular. He was naturally athletic, enjoyed sports and had a quick mind that helped him win many different kinds of games. Of all of George Washington's interests, one of his favorite things in the world was to work on his farm.

George Washington married a woman named Martha, who had been married before and already had a little boy and a little girl. He took Martha, and young Jacky and Patsy, to live with him at Mt. Vernon. Mt. Vernon was a beautiful, large plantation that had many smaller buildings besides the grand plantation house. Martha knew all about taking care of a large household. There were always a multitude of things going on at Mt. Vernon. The fields were full of crops that were carefully planted each season at just the right time. There were gardens full of lettuces, beans, tomatoes, herbs and more. There were cattle, beautiful race horses, chickens, pigs, cats and dogs. There were ponds full of fish and nurseries full of flowers. Orchards had bountiful peach and apple trees. Besides all of these things, there was a flour mill, blacksmith, brick kilns, carpenters, masons, weavers and shoemakers. George Washington rode throughout his land, telling the people to "buy nothing you can make yourselves." Six days a week, he woke early and worked hard all day. He loved to take off his handsome coat and help do the various kinds of hard work around the plantation. On Sundays, he rested, attended church, read to his children and talked to his wife. It was a beautiful and peaceful life at his favorite place in the world.

Not all of George Washington's life would end up being peaceful. Both George's father and his half-brother had served in the military. George Washington felt that a desire to fight for his country was part of his blood. Ever since he had been a small boy, he had been interested in battles and war. Before long, both his knowledge of the wilderness and his willingness to fight would be needed in order to help save his country.

Review Questions:

1. What kind of work did George Washington do when he was young?
2. Describe what Mt. Vernon was like.

Adventures in America Week 13

	Day 1	Day 2	Day 3
Reading	Read *Samuel Adams*	Read *The Boston Tea Party*	Read *Smart About* pg.25 and 21
Coloring/ Activity	"Punched Tin Pictures" activity	Coloring Page, pg. 61	Color Louisiana and Indiana on blank US map, pg. 2
Notebook	Narration from Read Aloud, history or reader, pg. 62	Copywork, pg. 63	Fill out notebook page for Louisiana and Indiana, pgs. 64, 65

Optional Read-Aloud:

The Courage of Sarah Noble
- Day 1: Chapter 1
- Day 2: Chapter 2
- Day 3: Chapter 3
- Day 4: Chapter 4
- Day 5: Chapter 5

Related Picture Books:

- *The Boston Tea Party* by Steven Kroll

Possible Reader:

- *The Josefina Story Quilt*, Coerr

Activity: Punched Tin Pictures

Tin was sometimes called the "Poor Man's Silver." Many people in colonial times could not afford silver decorations, but they often decorated tin to use as plates, wall hangings or lantern covers. Let your student give it a try!

Materials:
- Pencil, paper
- Old towel
- Aluminum foil pie plate
- Tape
- Thumbtack

• Draw a simple design on the paper that fits into the bottom of the plate. You might make a sun, flower, tree, etc.

• Tape the paper to the bottom of the pie plate.

• Place the towel on the tabletop to protect the surface as your student pokes holes with the thumbtack. Gently punch holes at regular intervals along the lines of your design.

• To hang, punch a hole in the top of the rim.

Optional Copywork: No taxation without representation!

Notes

Samuel Adams

Tensions were rising in the thirteen colonies. For years they had been ruled by the King of England, who lived across the ocean and had never been to America. Although many of the colonists loved King George III and were happy under his reign, there were more and more who grew dissatisfied. Those who were loyal to the Crown were called Loyalists or Torries. Men and women who had become upset by British rule were called Patriots or Whigs. One of the most vocal patriots in Boston was a man named Samuel Adams.

Samuel Adams had been passionately interested in politics since he was a young boy. He cared deeply about how the country was run and what rules or laws the people lived by. He loved to read books written by men with new ideas about words such as liberty, equality and rights. Over time he came to believe that all men had been created as equals and should not be ruled over unfairly by people who had been born into riches and power. He was a smart boy who did well in school. After studying hard and going to a very good college called Harvard, he tried his hand at various types of business. But no matter what jobs he tried to do, they just did not work out very well, and before long he had almost no money.

There was something that Samuel Adams did have plenty of, and that was passion! He grew more and more excited about politics and began to write about those wonderful ideas of liberty, equality and rights of the people. It turned out that writing was something that he did very well, and soon the people of Boston looked to Samuel Adams as a leader in politics. Soon there was plenty to write about, since King George was making the colonies pay more taxes.

The Colonists grew angry when tax laws such as the Sugar Act and the Stamp Act were passed. These laws meant that every time they bought certain goods at the store, they had to pay extra money to the King. They were not just upset about paying the money, they were not happy to be ruled by someone across the ocean who had no way of hearing about the Colonists' feelings and desires. A phrase became popular and was printed in newspapers, written on banners and shouted from mouths at political meetings: "No taxation without representation!" By this phrase, they meant that they should not be made to pay taxes when there was not anyone in England who was helping the King understand what the Colonists wanted. Of all the Patriots who were chanting this phrase, almost no voice was heard more often than that of Samuel Adams! "No taxation without representation!" He boomed loud and clear to whomever was listening.

Of course this greatly bothered the British soldiers in Boston, and soon King George himself had heard about Samuel Adams. Anxious to stop him, they offered him money if he would forget about his ideas of liberty. They knew he was desperately poor and that he certainly needed money. What they did not know was that Samuel Adams loved his country and freedom more than gold, and no amount of money would ever tempt him away from what he believed in: No taxation without representation!

Review Questions:

1. What was Samuel Adams passionate about?
2. Why were many of the Colonists unhappy to be under British rule?

The Boston Tea Party

King George III grew nervous. He knew he had to make those rebellious Patriots submit to his authority, or he was in danger of losing control in the colonies. He came up with a plan called the Tea Act. With the Tea Act, every time Colonists paid for their beloved English tea, they would also pay a tiny little tax. The tax was so low that tea would be cheaper than ever! But, by paying the tax, the Colonists would prove that they were loyal to the King. Surely they loved their tea and money more than the cause of liberty! This time, the King was sure they would obey.

In the end of November, a great ship named the Dartmouth sailed into Boston Harbor. Among its cargo were large crates full of tea leaves. Normally the ship's hold would be emptied quickly, with the boxes and barrels full of tea, cloth, spices and other merchandise divided among shopkeepers where it would be sold. Usually there were people anxiously awaiting the arrival of goods that had been sent from England, eager to buy the tea that they so dearly missed. This time, the Dartmouth was greeted by a stern-faced crowd. Colonists had already made their decision before the ship arrived. They would not pay the King's taxes on the tea, no matter what. In fact, the tea was forbidden to even come off of the ship.

That night, Samuel Adams called a meeting. He gathered together men called the Sons of Liberty. The Sons of Liberty were passionate about freedom and believed that men were equal. They wore silver medals around their necks, with a picture of a liberty tree engraved upon them. Samuel Adams knew he could count on these men to do their part to show the British soldiers just how serious the Patriots were about their cause. Besides the Sons of Liberty, there were thousands of other people at the meeting, all anxious to show their commitment to "No taxation without representation!" At the meeting, everyone agreed that the Dartmouth would have to return to England without unloading her stores of tea. In the days that followed, two more ships carrying tea arrived in the harbor.

Finally, it was the night before the Dartmouth would have to unload her tea so she could leave the Boston Harbor. Another meeting was called, but this time secret plans had already been made. Samuel Adams stood before the people and loudly spoke out, "This meeting can do nothing further to save the country." At these words, the Sons of Liberty dispersed. They quickly changed their clothes and put on disguises, many of them wearing face paint and carrying hatchets to look like Native Indians. In the darkness of the night, they slipped into the harbor and climbed into small boats, rowing silently and stealthily towards the three tea-bearing ships. Without making a noise, they boarded the large ships and informed the Captains that nothing on board would be harmed except the tea itself. Working quickly, they opened every single barrel and crate full of tea, emptying the contents into the water surrounding the ships. They made absolutely sure that not a tea leaf was spared, and that no other cargo was damaged. Once they had finished, they rowed their small boats back to land, took off their costumes, and pretended to have been soundly asleep in their beds all night. The precious English tea lay brewing in the waters of the harbor, and the event was soon named "The Boston Tea Party."

King George saw that the Colonists loved something more than tea or money: liberty!

Review Questions:

1. Why did the Colonists not want to buy the English tea?
2. What did the Sons of Liberty do at the Boston Tea Party?

Adventures in America Week 14

	Day 1	**Day 2**	**Day 3**
Reading	Read *Paul Revere*	Read *Midnight Ride of Paul Revere*	Read *Smart About* pg.31
Coloring/ Activity	Coloring Page, pg. 67	"Lantern Signals" activity	Color Mississippi on blank US map, pg. 2
Notebook	Narration from Read Aloud, history or reader, pg. 68	Copywork, pg. 69	Fill out notebook page for Mississippi, pg. 70

Optional Read-Aloud:

The Courage of Sarah Noble
- Day 1: Chapter 6
- Day 2: Chapter 7
- Day 3: Chapter 8
- Day 4: Chapter 9-10
- Day 5: Chapter 11

Related Picture Books:

- *Paul Revere's Ride* by Henry Wadsworth Longfellow, illustrations by Ted Rand

Possible Reader:

- *The Josefina Story Quilt*, Coerr

Activity: Lantern Signals
Materials:
-Flashlight

•Discuss with your student how Paul Revere had followed a plan using lanterns as signals in the church tower.

•Come up with your own signals to use within your family. (i.e. One flash from flashlight means it's time to eat dinner, two flashes means the dog wants to go out, etc.)

•Use your flash signals whenever possible over the next few days.

Optional Copywork: The Minute Men waited anxiously for any important news.

Notes

Paul Revere

Boston was full of quiet pride and joy after the unforgettable night of the Tea Party in the harbor. Nobody admitted to having had anything to do with it, of course. It was a great secret, and the whole town was talking about nothing else.

A silversmith named Paul Revere had led one of the groups of men on board the ships. Paul Revere was a trusted leader and messenger within the Patriot society. His normal job was to create beautiful things out of silver, such as bowls, plates and decorations. Besides being a skilled silversmith, he was also a master engraver. An engraver is someone who cuts designs onto materials like wood or metal. Paul Revere's father had come to Boston to learn the trade of silversmithing, and then had taught his son after him. After his father died, Paul ran the family silver shop in his place. Paul was married and had many children. He had to work very hard in order to support his large family.

While most of his days were spent laboring over silver in his workshop, his evenings and spare moments were dedicated to the cause of liberty. Riding on his horse, he would travel from Boston out to the different towns that dotted the countryside, delivering important messages and information about the British troops. The British soldiers marched up and down the streets of Boston in their beautiful red coats, and Paul Revere and others listened carefully in order to hear what their plans were. Many young boys and girls acted as spies, listening to the conversation of the redcoats and reporting back to men like Samuel Adams. Samuel Adams would then have Paul Revere ride out to tell the Minute Men what had been heard.

The Minute Men waited anxiously to hear any important news. They were called "Minute Men" because they were prepared to fight night or day at a moment's notice. These handpicked men were usually young, tall and strong. They had practiced using weapons and were skilled with their muskets. Of all the fighting men in the country and towns, these were the ones who would be first at the scenes of battle. They loved their country and were passionately dedicated to liberty, eager to do all they could and even lay down their lives for the cause.

One day in April the word came that the British soldiers were planning to leave Boston soon. It was quite suspicious. Horses were groomed and preparations were made. There was no doubt that they were planning on making a move, but people were unsure exactly what the move would be. They suspected an attack on Concord, a town that held large stores of military supplies and weapons. If they were in fact headed to Concord and going right past the town of Lexington, then Samuel Adams and John Hancock would need to be forewarned. They were both staying at a house in Lexington, and two such important leaders to the Cause must be protected. The Minute Men must also be warned in time to meet the redcoats as they came. The obvious choice of a messenger was Paul Revere. They began to form a plan…

Review Questions:

1. What was Paul Revere's job?
2. What were the Minute Men ready to do?

Midnight Ride of Paul Revere

The British were surely preparing to move the troops, and someone needed to ride ahead and sound the alarm. Still, no one was sure whether they would leave by boat across the Charles River or over the land. Paul Revere and his friend, William Dawes, were chosen to deliver the warnings to the towns and houses along the countryside. They would start in separate places and take two different routes in order to alert the Minute Men and the farmers along the way. A plan was made.

There happened to be a church with a tall belfry, or bell tower, that could be seen from across the river. The sexton of the church would watch and wait to see whether the troops would leave by land or "by sea," meaning across the river. If they were choosing the land route, he would light one lantern and hold it up in the window of the belfry. If he saw the redcoats boarding boats and preparing to cross the river, he would light two lanterns instead.

Paul Revere silently rowed his own little boat across the river without being noticed by anyone. He stood at the edge of the water, holding the reigns of his horse and eagerly watching for the signal. Night had fallen and the only light came from the moon and stars above. Nothing could be seen in the belfry of the Old North Church. He squinted his eyes and looked closely. Minutes ticked by as Paul Revere anxiously watched. Finally, there appeared the glimmer of a tiny light across the water. It was coming from the church belfry! For a moment there was just the one lantern, but soon another shone next to it. Two lanterns! The redcoats were crossing the water! Without hesitating a second longer, Paul Revere swung up into the seat of his saddle and urged his horse on. Riding like the wind, they flew away from Boston and galloped through all of Middlesex County.

Avoiding the houses of men known to be loyal to the King, he carried his message to all the farmers and Minute Men who would fight for liberty. He shouted the phrase "The Regulars are coming!" As men heard the warning, they quickly dressed and prepared their weapons. Some jumped on their own horses, riding in all directions to alert friends and neighbors. Eventually, Paul Revere reached Lexington, where Samuel Adams and John Hancock were staying. These two important men discussed together and planned what to do next.

Paul Revere rode on to Concord, but was captured by British troops along the way. It did not matter; he had done his job well. By the time the redcoats reached Concord, a makeshift army of young and old farmers had joined with the Minute Men and were ready to fight. They may not have had the beautiful uniforms that the British soldiers wore, the shiny new weapons or the years of military training. They had something else that allowed them to fight and take the victory, and that was a love for liberty and a desire to defend their homes and land. Their courage brought them together and made them a serious threat to the British troops, who ended up traveling back to Boston. The King's soldiers were amazed by the fierce fighting that a group of untrained farmers had done!

Review Questions:

1. What was the warning signal from the church that had been planned ahead of time?
2. What was the reason for Paul Revere's midnight ride?

Adventures in America Week 15

	Day 1	Day 2	Day 3
Reading	Read *Declaration of Independence, Part 1*	Read *Declaration of Independence, Part 2*	Read *Smart About* pg.20 and 8
Coloring/ Activity	Coloring Page, pg. 71	"Declaration Scroll" activity	Color Illinois and Alabama on blank US map, pg. 2
Notebook	Narration from Read Aloud, history or reader, pg. 72	Copywork, pg. 73	Fill out notebook page for Illinois and Alabama, pgs. 74, 75

Optional Read-Aloud:

The Matchlock Gun
- Day 1: Chapter 1
- Day 2: Chapter 2
- Day 3: Chapter 3
- Day 4: Chapter 4
- Day 5: Chapter 5

Related Picture Books:

- *The 4th of July Story* by Alice Dalgliesh

Possible Reader:

- *Red, White and Blue*, Herman

Activity: Declaration Scroll

Materials:
-Paper   -Marker or calligraphy pen
-Ribbon

•Make your own "Declaration of Independence." After reading or paraphrasing the first paragraph of the actual document and discussing the meaning, ask your student what they would like written on their declaration. They might wish to summarize the actual one, or to be creative and write something completely different. Act as their scribe and write their words in fancy letters on the paper. Put the date at the top, as in the real one.

•Have family members read and sign their names under the declaration. Roll up and tie with a ribbon.

•Your student may enjoy ceremoniously standing in front of the family, unrolling the document and reading or summarizing its contents.

Optional Copywork: It was July 4th, 1776, and a country had been born!

Notes

Declaration of Independence, Part 1

Ever since the first shots had been fired in Concord, the British army and the American colonies were at war. George Washington, the wealthy plantation owner from Virginia, was appointed as General over the American army. Although inexperienced, he was a wise leader and was loved and admired by his soldiers. His army was made up of all kinds of men. There were very old men who had lived through other wars. There were boys as young as ten years old, helping out all they could. There were white and black men, rich and poor men. It was a common cause that brought them together from farms and towns all over the colonies. They all loved freedom and would do anything to defend it.

While most of the men were gathered on the battlefield, there were others who had a different kind of important work to do. Men from each of the thirteen colonies regularly met together in Congress to decide what the future of America should be. One by one, the men told how they had had enough of British rule! They were tired of the taxes, the strict laws, the soldiers marching throughout their land. One by one, they became convinced of one thing: they needed to break away from England and King George III! They should become their own country.

A man named Thomas Jefferson was given a very important job. He was chosen to write a document that would tell about how America wanted to be free from English rule. It would be called the Declaration of Independence.

This was not an easy task because each and every word had to be considered carefully. Thomas Jefferson rented two rooms, a parlor and a bedroom at the Graff House in Philadelphia. He bent over his desk, writing and re-writing for almost three weeks. Finally, he was pleased with the words. Benjamin Franklin and a man named John Adams read what Jefferson had written. "Wonderful," they both said. But they did have changes to make. Most of the words were scratched out and re-written yet again. Finally, the men were happy with it and took it to Congress.

Men from the different colonies read the words. They made a few changes here and a few changes there before they were all satisfied.

With great flourish, a man named John Hancock lifted his pen and signed his name, large and clear, right in the center under the Declaration of Independence. The other men picked up their pens and added their own names. It was July 4th, 1776, and a country had been born! The United States of America celebrated its first birthday on that fourth of July!

One of the sentences in the document read "We hold these truths to be self-evident, that all men are created equal, that they are endowed by their Creator with certain unalienable Rights, that among these are Life, Liberty and the pursuit of Happiness." That meant that men everywhere should be free. That sentence was like a little seed that was planted into fertile ground and grew into a strong, tall oak tree. However, instead of just a tree, it was a country that grew, strong and free.

Review Questions:

1. Who wrote the Declaration of Independence?
2. When is America's birthday?

Declaration of Independence, Part 2

Fourteen year old Henry was an apprentice at a printer's shop in Philadelphia. His master, Mr. John Dunlap, usually printed newspapers. Mr. Dunlap loved to talk about the cause of liberty and people's rights, and he also loved to help do his part in the fight for freedom. He had even fought in a troop led by General George Washington! On the afternoon of July 4, John Hancock appeared at his shop with orders to print a special document. He carefully unrolled the scroll and saw the words "Declaration of Independence" written at the top.

Swallowing a lump in his throat, Mr. Dunlap looked up with tears shining in his eyes. "The time has come. The time has come," he said, looking at something past Henry and far away.

"They will need hundreds of these! Make haste!" Mr. Dunlap was immediately all business again, setting type and getting it just right for this important job. Henry worked energetically, helping Mr. Dunlap all he could. They printed copy after copy of the declaration, working after the sun had set and darkness had fallen over Philadelphia. They were fully aware of the extreme importance of this document. It must be handled perfectly.

At long last the copies were finished and laid neatly on a beautiful wooden table in the office. Mr. Dunlap had ordered Henry to shine the table until the wood shone before he was willing to place such precious items upon it. Henry had rubbed again and again with his cloth, smiling to himself. He knew that he was fortunate to play a small part in helping America become her very own country. "The United States of America," he whispered quietly, testing out the sound of the words. The name sounded brave, strong and beautiful. A thrill went up his spine.

In the distance, sunlight was gleaming on the horizon. Slowly the darkness of night was chased away by the bright July sun. Messengers pulled up to the print shop on horseback, waiting to receive copies of the declaration. Each was handed a bundle of the precious papers. With an urging on of "Godspeed!" by the few onlookers, they were off! They would carry the declaration to each of the thirteen colonies, where it would be publicly read to townspeople and troops.

Within the town of Philadelphia herself, a man named Colonel John Nixon stood at the State House and "proclaimed," or read, the declaration. His voice rang out with the words "We hold these truths to be self-evident, that all men are created equal, that they are endowed by their Creator with certain unalienable Rights, that among these are Life, Liberty and the pursuit of Happiness." Cheers, hurrahs and even firings of muskets accompanied the words, as the townspeople burst into exuberant celebration. Throughout the city, bells rang constantly all day long. Mr. Dunlap looked on in patriotic pride.

Review Questions:

1. How was the Declaration of Independence carried to the other colonies?
2. What happened when the declaration was first read in Philadelphia?

Adventures in America Week 16

	Day 1	Day 2	Day 3
Reading	Read *The Liberty Bell*	Read *Betsy Ross*	Read *Smart About* pg.26
Coloring/ Activity	Coloring Page, pg. 77	"Five Point Star" activity	Color Maine on blank US map, pg. 2
Notebook	Narration from Read Aloud, history or reader, pg. 78	Copywork, pg. 79	Fill out notebook page for Maine, pg. 80

Optional Read-Aloud:

The Matchlock Gun
- Day 1: Chapter 6
- Day 2: Chapter 7
- Day 3: Chapter 8
- Day 4: Chapter 9
- Day 5: Chapter 10

Related Picture Books:

- *The 4th of July Story* by Alice Dalgliesh

Possible Reader:

- *Red, White and Blue*, Herman

Activity: Five Point Star
Materials:
-Red, white and blue paper   -Scissors

•Trim your pieces of paper so that they are 8 ½ by 10 inches (not 11).

•There are many websites with clear pictures and instructions about how to fold and cut a five point star. Since websites change so often, I suggest you do a search on "five point star."

•Follow the instructions and make as many stars as your student desires.

•You may wish to hang your stars from a mobile. You can also decorate them with glitter.

Optional Copywork: For years the loud, clear ring of the Liberty Bell would chime out to the people of Philadelphia.

Notes

The Liberty Bell

In the important city of Philadelphia there was a very important building. It was called the State House. Inside this building, men from every colony would meet to talk about problems and try to find good answers. Today you can see a picture of the State House on the back of an American hundred dollar bill. It is made of red bricks and has a steeple which points up to the sky.

Behind the State House was a nice tree with a long, sturdy branch. On this branch hung a special bell that William Penn had brought with him from England. Whenever a meeting was about to begin or an important announcement had to be made, William Penn's bell would ring and the townspeople would hear it. Storekeepers would leave their stores, bakers would leave their bakeries and carpenters would leave their workbenches. They all wanted to hear the latest news. Maybe a new shipment from England had arrived. Maybe a new tax law had been passed by King George. Everyone was curious to know just what the bell had to say.

Soon a shiny, new bell tower was being built up on the State House, and someone suggested that it ought to have a shiny, new bell to hang from it. Everyone thought that was a wonderful idea! After all, the little bell on the tree was not quite loud enough and was certainly not large enough for such an important building in one of America's most important cities! It was agreed that the finest bell would be made from the finest materials. They immediately wrote a letter to England, requesting that a nice bell be made and sent on a ship sailing to Pennsylvania. A Bible verse was chosen to be cast onto the bell, "Proclaim LIBERTY throughout all the land unto all the inhabitants thereof." (Leviticus 25:10)

Months passed and soon it was summer in Philadelphia. The city held its breath as it waited expectantly for a ship to arrive carrying their precious bell. Finally, on one warm August day a ship called "The Matilda" came to the docks. Cries of "Hear Ye, Hear Ye, the bell has come!" were heard by the whole town, and everyone rushed to see. The bell was carefully carried to the State House, and a day was set for the first ring.

Statesmen, Quakers, wives, children, teachers and more gathered together to listen to the bell's first chime. It rang out pure, loud and clear! And then…CRACK! Before it could ring again, a long crack appeared. What had happened to their beautiful bell? Never mind, they said, we'll fix it!

Making a bell was like following a recipe. You needed to have just the right amounts of copper and brass. They melted down the bell and added even more copper, hoping this time the bell would be stronger. Once the bell was re-cast, a celebratory picnic was planned for a second ringing of the bell. Yet again the townspeople gathered in anticipation. "RRRIIIIIING!" Oh, it sounded dreadful! Hands went over ears and people looked on in disappointment. The extra copper must have horribly changed the sound of the bell. Well, it would just have to be made again.

This time the ingredients were carefully measured out and it was re-cast into a beautiful looking and beautiful sounding bell. Without a public celebration, it was hung quietly in the State House belfry. For years and years, the loud, clear ring of the Liberty Bell would chime out and announce to the people of Philadelphia any important news. One day, more than fifty years later the bell would crack once more and never ring again. However, before that day it rang out some of the most significant events in America's history. Today it is one of our country's best known symbols and the crack only makes it more dearly loved.

Review Questions:

1. Where was the Liberty Bell hung?
2. What happened to the Liberty Bell?

Betsy Ross

As a young girl, Betsy loved to sew! Her sisters preferred embroidery or knitting, but Betsy just wanted to sew. She enjoyed putting tiny, straight stitches on their plain Quaker sheets and clothing. Her mother taught Betsy all she knew. She even taught her how to fold a square piece of fabric and cut it into a five pointed star, instead of the normal six pointed stars that everyone else made. People from all around acknowledged her skill and often gave her little tasks to work on.

Betsy felt special, but not just because she was good with her needle and thread. She felt important because she had a very special twin. Not the normal kind of a twin, like a brother or a sister. She had a twin that had been born the same year as she had in Philadelphia. Her twin hung beautiful and proud from the State House belfry, which her father had helped to build. Yes, her twin was the beloved Liberty Bell! As a newborn baby, Betsy had been carried along with her older brothers and sisters to watch the bell as it was first rung, as it cracked, and as it was next rung. She felt that there was a special bond between her and that great bell which "proclaimed liberty through all the land."

Betsy grew up and met the handsome John Ross. John thought Betsy was sweet and pretty, along with being talented at sewing. He asked her to marry him, and she said yes. It was an exciting time! Everywhere was talk of freedom and independence. More and more people grew unhappy with being English colonies. There were dreams of forming a new, independent nation ruled by Americans instead of by a King across the ocean. Soon, John Ross went to fight in the war for freedom and Betsy was left alone to run their upholstery store.

John Ross had an uncle, Colonel Ross, who fought alongside General George Washington. One day, George Washington mentioned to the Colonel that he thought there ought to be one flag that all the soldiers from all the colonies could carry bravely into battle. Until then, each colony held its own flag and it was hard to tell who was from where. Colonel Ross agreed that one flag was just what America needed, and he knew just the girl to sew it for them.

Betsy Ross opened the door of their upholstery shop one morning to see the tall figure of General George Washington on her doorstep. 'Would she be willing to sew a flag for the thirteen colonies?' he asked. 'It would be a tremendous honor,' she replied. He showed her a sketch of the flag. It would have thirteen stripes for the thirteen colonies, red and white. In the top corner would be thirteen six pointed stars shining in a circle against a bright blue background. Betsy agreed that the design was beautiful, but asked whether they might like five pointed stars instead? She quickly folded a piece of paper again and again. With just one snip, she had a star with straight edges and five clean points. That would be just the thing! George Washington gladly left Betsy to work sewing the flag.

Soon, not only did American soldiers all have the same red, white and blue banner to carry, but every home, store and building also displayed the flag proudly. It seems fitting that it was sewn by a girl born the same year as the Liberty Bell, since both the bell and the flag inspire pride in the hearts of Americans.

Review Questions:

1. What contribution (new idea) did Betsy Ross add to the design of the first flag?
2. What did the first flag look like?

Adventures in America Week 17

	Day 1	Day 2	Day 3
Reading	Read *George Washington's Daring Move*	Read *Winter at Valley Forge*	Read *Smart About* pg.32 and 11
Coloring/ Activity	Coloring Page, pg. 81	"Make Berry Dye" activity	Color Missouri and Arkansas on blank US map, pg. 2
Notebook	Narration from Read Aloud, history or reader, pg. 82	Copywork, pg. 83	Fill out notebook page for Missouri and Arkansas, pgs. 84, 85

Optional Read-Aloud:

Tolliver's Secret
- Day 1: Chapter 1
- Day 2: Pg.16-Middle Pg.23
- Day 3: Pg.23-31
- Day 4: Chapter 3
- Day 5: Chapter 4

Related Picture Books:

- *Winter at Valley Forge: Survival and Victory* by James Knight

Possible Reader:

- *Wagon Wheels*, Brenner

Optional Copywork: Winters were always very hard for soldiers, and this one was no different.

Activity: Make Berry Dye

Colonial people made most of their own clothes and used dyes made from objects found in nature. Let your student dye fabric the colonial way!

Materials:
-1/2 cup salt
-3 cups of any kind of berry (cherries, strawberries, blueberries, raspberries, etc.)
-6 cups water   -100% cotton white tee shirt (you
-8 cups water   could also do white socks, etc.)

•Combine 8 c. of water and salt. Bring to boil. Lower heat, add tee shirt. Let soak in simmering water for one hour. This acts as a fixative for the dye. At same time:

•Coarsely chop or mash berries. Combine berries and 6 c. water in large pot. Bring to a boil, lower heat and simmer for one hour.

•Remove shirt from salt solution. Rinse thoroughly in cold water.

•Strain berries from liquid. Place tee shirt in dye. Let soak (the longer it soaks, the brighter the color will be).

•Wring shirt (you may want to wear gloves to avoid staining your skin) and hang to dry. Always wash separately in cold water!

Notes

George Washington's Daring Move

Soon after that first 4th of July, General George Washington read the Declaration of Independence to the men in his army. They listened eagerly. The words inspired the men and strengthened their courage. They were not just defending their homes and land; they were defending a country: the United States of America. It was definitely something worth fighting for! They knew that unless they won this war against England, all talk of independence would mean nothing. They still had battles to fight.

As the months passed, the men grew more and more discouraged. So far, the British troops were better trained, had more weapons, better uniforms and more food. The redcoats seemed to be winning. While they had beautiful, matching uniforms and shiny boots, many of the American soldiers were barefoot. They were also sick. Whenever one of the men became sick, his sickness was sure to spread to those around him. Before long, most of the soldiers were too sick to do much fighting, and General Washington grew worried. Christmas was fast approaching and a bitterly cold winter would follow. How could he inspire his troops to stay brave and continue fighting the war? He came up with a daring and brave plan.

The American troops and British troops were separated by the Delaware River. Once the Americans had crossed over the water, General Washington had made sure that there were no boats anywhere for sixty miles. It would be almost impossible for the redcoats to cross over and attack them. He found out that across the river, in the town of Trenton, there was an army full of Hessian soldiers. The Hessians were fighting for England, but they were actually from Germany. King George had promised to pay the Hessians if they would leave Germany and sail to America to help him win the war. There were more than a thousand of these Hessians in Trenton at Christmas time.

General Washington only told a few men of his plan because he wanted to keep it secret from the enemy. He told each of his men to carry enough food for three days and lots of powder for their muskets. On Christmas night, they headed towards the Delaware River. There were large flat boats waiting to take the soldiers across. It was difficult to load all the men, the horses and the cannons, but soon they were all floating across the river. The water was freezing cold with chunks of ice floating in it. The men were chilled by the air. Suddenly, it began to storm! Not only rain, but snow and sleet blew in huge gusts against the men. It seemed like forever, but they finally reached the other side of the river. Without making a sound, the soldiers left the boats and carried their weapons across nine miles of countryside before reaching Trenton.

In Trenton, the Hessians were enjoying a Christmas party with plenty of food and drinks. They went to bed very late at night, exhausted after the parties. By the time the sun rose the next morning, every street in town was filled with American soldiers! The Hessians were taken completely by surprise. They fought for a while, but soon gave up. About one thousand Hessian soldiers were taken as prisoners back across the Delaware River with General Washington! His army was now full of hope and courage after the success of his daring plan.

Review Questions:

1. What were the German soldiers who fought for England called?
2. What was the name of the river that Washington led his men across?

Winter at Valley Forge

After General Washington had managed to capture so many Hessian prisoners, his troops were happy and full of hope about the war. They were quite sure that America would indeed be able to win her freedom from English rule. After all, they thought, surely no one had ever fought so bravely as Washington's army! Over the next year there were other battles. It seemed that the redcoats were just too many, too well trained and too smart. The American soldiers started to wonder whether they really could win this war.

Soon it was winter again, and General Washington looked for a place to set up winter quarters. At that time, most armies took a break from fighting during the coldest months of winter. Washington chose a nice place near a river called Valley Forge. It would be just the place for the troops to rest and practice before fighting again in the Spring. Just before Christmas, twelve thousand men marched together and began building log huts to live in. Soon, Valley Forge was full of small cabins that would shelter the men throughout the long winter months.

Winters were always very hard for soldiers, and this one was no different. There was never much food to eat because meat was so hard to find. Most days the men ate tasteless bread called "firecakes." The firecakes were made from flour mixed with some water. Without any salt to flavor the dough, they were bland and unappetizing. Clothing was also a problem for the men. After marching so many miles and fighting so many battles, their shoes were worn completely through. Some men wore their tattered boots, but others were barefoot except for pieces of cloth wrapped around their feet. In warmer weather, that would have been difficult on their feet, but in the freezing temperatures it became painful and dangerous. Many uniforms were threadbare and full of holes, barely covering the men at all. To make things even worse, they became sick. As soon as one man became sick, his sickness usually spread to the others near him. Soon thousands of men were ill with diseases.

General Washington became worried. He knew that he needed a strong, healthy army to fight the British. Thankfully, help came in different forms.

A group of people called Camp Followers came to offer any help they could to the poor soldiers. This group was made up of the wives, children, mothers and sisters of the fighting men. They worked at washing uniforms, sewing and mending holes, preparing food and cheering up the men. A Prussian man from Europe, named von Steuben, came with a letter from Benjamin Franklin. He knew how to train soldiers and was coming to help. General Washington gave him a group of one hundred men to train. Every day, von Steuben taught them how to line up, fire their muskets and fight skillfully. Before long, these men were well trained and they each began to teach others. Soon, General Washington's army was well prepared for the battles to come.

Eventually the cold winter snows melted away and there was more food and warm sunshine to lift the men's spirits. It had been difficult, but the army had shown again that they had courage and would stay true to the cause of liberty, no matter what came their way.

Review Questions:

1. What were some of the difficulties the men faced during the winter at Valley Forge?
2. Who were some of the people that came to help the soldiers?

Adventures in America Week 18

	Day 1	Day 2	Day 3
Reading	Read *Molly Pitcher*	Read *Yorktown and Victory*	Read *Smart About* pg.29
Coloring/ Activity	Coloring Page, pg. 87	"War Drum" activity	Color Michigan on blank US map, pg. 2
Notebook	Narration from Read Aloud, history or reader, pg. 88	Copywork, pg. 89	Fill out notebook page for Michigan, pg. 90

Optional Read-Aloud:

Tolliver's Secret
• Day 1: Chapter 5
• Day 2: Chapter 6
• Day 3: Chapter 7
• Day 4: Chapter 8
• Day 5: Pg.107-bottom of Pg.112

Related Picture Books:

• *If You Lived at the Time of the American Revolution* by Kay Moore

Possible Reader:

• *Wagon Wheels*, Brenner

Optional Copywork: In addition to the many brave men who fought for America's liberty, there were just as many courageous women who did their part.

Activity: War Drum
Materials:
-Empty coffee can or oatmeal canister   -Yarn
-Two sheets of red construction paper   -Glue, scissors
-One sheet of white or tan colored felt   -Hole punch
-Wooden chopsticks or dowels for drumsticks

•Remove lid from container and set aside. Punch one hole at top of each side of the container. Trim the construction paper to fit around canister. Your student may wish to decorate the paper at this point.

•Cover the canister with glue, and press the paper onto the container. Poke through the construction paper where the holes are. Poke a long piece of yarn through holes and tie to be a strap for your student to carry the drum around his/ her neck.

•Apply glue all over top of lid, and around the edges. Turn lid glue side down onto felt. Use scissors to trim around the lid, leaving at least a half inch border.

•Place felt-covered lid onto container and put rubber band around felt, pulling the felt tight.

•Have fun marching and playing your drum with the chopsticks!

Notes

Molly Pitcher

In addition to the many brave men who fought for America's liberty, there were just as many courageous women who did their part. It was the wives, mothers, daughters and sisters who gave up their normal duties to sew uniforms and make bandages for wounded soldiers. While the men went away to fight battles, women stayed home and made sure the fields were planted and the land was kept safe. The war required just as much bravery and hard work from the women, as they supported their men and the cause with all their hearts. Several stories of heroines have survived through the years and show us a few examples of incredible courage. One of these stories is about a woman we now call Molly Pitcher, although she used to be known as Mary Ludwig.

Mary Ludwig was born and raised on a dairy farm in New Jersey. She knew all about hard work and was often busy helping her parents with their chores. She never did learn to read or write, but she learned all about taking care of a farm. When she was just a young teenager, she met a barber named William Hays. Soon they were married. They did not have much money, but they worked hard and loved one another. Before long, William Hays chose to join the American army and help fight the redcoats in the war for independence. He traveled to Valley Forge, where the men were camping for the winter. Mary decided to go along and join him there. She thought that there just might be something she could do to help her husband and her country.

At Valley Forge, Mary joined the Camp Followers. She helped bake and deliver food to the men, wash clothes and blankets, and nurse sick soldiers. It was hard work, but Mary was used to hard work and did not mind. She was happy to be able to help. The Prussian man, von Steuben, came to train the men, and William was soon working hard learning from him. Mary and some others helped by bringing water to the thirsty men while they were drilling with their guns. William and the soldiers were grateful and would often call out for water. A common nickname for Mary was Molly, and so they would usually call her Molly. When asking for a drink from the pitcher they would yell out, "Molly! Pitcher!" Soon she became known among the men as Molly Pitcher.

After the men had left Valley Forge, there was a battle at a place called Monmouth. Molly found a spring nearby and carried water from the spring to the hot and thirsty fighting men. Her husband, William, was busy at work loading a cannon. Soon, he was wounded and had to be carried off of the battlefield. Molly set down her pitcher and took her husband's place at the cannon! For the rest of the day, she worked tirelessly at loading the cannon in the middle of heavy fire. It was an astounding act of bravery and service to her country, and we still remember her to this day.

Review Questions:

1. How did Molly Pitcher get her nickname?
2. How did Molly Pitcher help the soldiers?

Yorktown and Victory

After the men had been so well trained by von Steuben at Valley Forge, they began to fight better than they had ever fought before! At first, King George had assumed that this would be an easy war for England to win. By now, he was beginning to realize that George Washington was a stronger enemy than he had thought. Still, George Washington did need help if he was going to win the war, and that help came from France.

Benjamin Franklin had taken a special trip across the ocean to France. The people of France also loved liberty and freedom, just like the Americans did. They sincerely hoped that America would win her independence from England. After many discussions, Benjamin Franklin finally persuaded them to send troops over to America to help fight the British. Once they arrived, Washington's army was stronger and larger than ever before.

George Washington knew that the British army was camped near a place called Yorktown in Virginia. He came up with a cunning plan. The French armies surrounded Yorktown on one side, and George Washington's men were on the other. There was no way out for the British. George Washington himself fired the first gun!

After three days of battle, the redcoats began to run out of ammunition for their guns. They were exhausted from the fight. Finally, one cool morning in October, a single drummer came out from the British side. He beat his drum as he marched towards the American army. A soldier was following behind the drummer. In his hand was a small white flag that he was waving back and forth. A white flag meant surrender. The redcoats were giving up the fight. They knew they had been beaten, and this was the end. The British soldiers laid down their guns before the Americans. Many were in tears over their loss. Eventually, England signed a treaty saying that America was indeed independent. All of the British troops were sent back to England, and the war was officially over.

Many had thought the day would never come. Many had doubted that an army made up of farmers and ordinary men could ever beat an army of trained, professional soldiers. But led by the inspiring beliefs of men like Samuel Adams, Thomas Jefferson and Benjamin Franklin, Americans had fought bravely for what they held to be true. "All men are created equal, that they are endowed by their Creator with certain unalienable Rights, that among these are Life, Liberty and the pursuit of Happiness." They had accomplished a wonderful dream of a new country, free and independent!

Review Questions:

1. What happened at the Battle of Yorktown?
2. Who won the Revolutionary War between England and America?

Adventures in America Week 19

	Day 1	**Day 2**	**Day 3**
Reading	Read *We the People*	Read *President George Washington*	Read *Smart About* pg.16
Coloring/ Activity	Coloring Page, pg. 91	"Cotton Ball Powdered Wig" activity	Color Florida on blank US map, pg. 2
Notebook	Narration from Read Aloud, history or reader, pg. 92	Copywork, pg. 93	Fill out notebook page for Florida, pg. 94

Optional Read-Aloud:

Tolliver's Secret
- Day 1: Pg.112-Pg.122
- Day 2: Chapter 10
- Day 3: Chapter 11
- Day 4: Chapter 12
- Day 5: Chapter 13

Related Picture Books:

- *A More Perfect Union: The Story of Our Constitution* by Betsy Maestro

Possible Reader:

- *Wagon Train*, Kramer

Activity: Cotton Ball Powdered Wig
Materials:
-Small paper lunch bag (white if possible)
-Cotton balls   -Scissors, pencil glue

•Place the bag over child's head and trace the forehead and head area with a pencil.

•Remove bag and cut out the head shape to use as the base for your wig.

•Glue cotton balls to completely cover the paper (stretching them out covers the area nicely). Let dry.

•Take a picture of your child wearing their own powdered wig- just like the Founding Fathers!

Optional Copywork: The Constitution would help the thirteen states come together as one nation.

Notes

We the People

Finally, the Revolutionary War was finished! America was truly her own country, made up of thirteen different states. The Declaration of Independence had proclaimed her free, but there was still not a set of rules saying how the country ought to be run. What was needed was another document, called a Constitution, that would describe what laws and rules the states would have. This would help the thirteen states come together as one nation.

Men from each of the states came together for a special meeting. Important heroes of the Revolution were there, like Benjamin Franklin and George Washington. Many of the men had fought in the war, and several had even signed the Declaration of Independence. They were some of the bravest and smartest men in the country, and they cared deeply about protecting the freedoms they had fought for. One man, named James Madison, helped lead the meetings. Today he is called the "Father of the Constitution." Each state had different ideas about how the country should be run. It took a long time and plenty of discussion before they were able to agree. Finally, they began to write out the Constitution. Every single word and sentence was talked about until at last almost everyone was happy with it.

The Constitution described how the president of the United States should be elected, what he was allowed to do, how laws would be made, and how Congress would work. Most importantly, it set up a government that would place power in the hands of the people. Instead of being ruled by one all powerful king or ruler, the people would choose their own president and vote for laws to be passed. The United States of America was the first nation in the world to create such a government.

Once the Constitution was written, it was time for the men from each state to sign it. The only state that was not present was Rhode Island. As the men solemnly watched, George Washington picked up a quill pen and signed his name. The first signature was fittingly made by the man who had led American troops to victory and freedom! Thirty-eight men followed by signing their names.

The men who wrote and signed the Constitution are called the Founding Fathers of the United States. Today, the "sons and daughters" of the Founding Fathers still enjoy the freedoms that these men worked so hard to protect. The beginning part of the Constitution is called the Preamble, and it goes like this, "We the People of the United States, in order to form a more perfect Union, establish Justice, insure domestic Tranquility, provide for the common defense, promote the general Welfare, and secure the Blessings of Liberty to ourselves and our Posterity, do ordain and establish this Constitution for the United States of America."

Review Questions:

1. Who was the first man to sign the Constitution?
2. What do we call the men who wrote and signed the Constitution?

President George Washington

George Washington had already done much to serve his country. He had left his beloved farm at Mt. Vernon to lead the American army for six long years. Finally the war for Independence had been won! George Washington had led the troops to victory! Now, he longed to return to his home. He missed walking through the fields and orchards at his plantation. He missed spending quiet evenings at home in his beautiful house, with his wife, Martha, at his side. He missed leisurely reading books from his large, private library. Surely, he deserved to retire in peace.

On the other side of the Atlantic Ocean, King George III heard of George Washington's plans to return to Mt. Vernon. The King was astounded. He said, "If he does that, he will be the greatest man in the world!" He said that because he knew that most men love power, especially the men who lead armies. He expected that George Washington would use the troops to stay in control of the country. However, he was mistaken! George Washington surprised the King of England by quietly returning to his home once the fighting was finished. He loved freedom much more than he loved power! His greatest desire was that power would be left in the hands of the people.

It soon became obvious that America needed some changes, and George Washington left home yet again to help write and sign the Constitution. After the Constitution was signed, the Founding Fathers thought about what kind of a man they should elect as president to lead the United States of America. Without a single hesitation or doubt, the men from every State agreed that the best man for the job was George Washington! Although George and his wife Martha would have preferred to stay in their home and lead quiet lives, they knew it was more important to do what was best for their country. They packed up their clothes and some books, and traveled to New York City.

Standing on a high balcony of Federal Hall, George Washington gazed out over the throngs that had gathered to see him. Solemnly, he raised his right hand. He promised the people that he would do his best as president of the United States, and that he would protect the Constitution. He gave a speech to the crowd, which was called an inaugural address. Ever since that first speech, every single American president has also begun their presidency with an inaugural address. George Washington was president for eight years, which was two terms. At the end of his second term, he decided that he would not be president again. His decision led to the tradition that no president would serve more than two terms. Yet again, King George III had been proven wrong. Here was a man who loved the rights and freedom of his country more than power for himself.

At long last, George and Martha were free to retire and lead normal, quiet lives at Mt. Vernon. In just a few years, George Washington became ill and died. The entire nation was grief-stricken, and they mourned him for months. He was given the nickname of "Father of our Country." Some special words were spoken about him at his funeral, saying that George Washington was "First in war, first in peace, and first in the hearts of his countrymen." To this day, he remains one of the greatest presidents that the United States has ever had!

Review Questions:

1. Why was King George III surprised to hear George Washington talk about returning home?
2. How many terms did George Washington serve as president of the United States?

Adventures in America Week 20

	Day 1	Day 2	Day 3
Reading	Read *Abigail Adams, Part 1*	Read *Abigail Adams, Part 2*	Read *Smart About* pg.50
Coloring/ Activity	Coloring Page, pg. 95	"Spoon Doll" activity	Color Texas on blank US map, pg. 2
Notebook	Narration from Read Aloud, history or reader, pg. 96	Copywork, pg. 97	Fill out notebook page for Texas, pg. 98

Optional Read-Aloud:

The Cabin Faced West
- Day 1: Chapter 1
- Day 2: Chapter 2
- Day 3: Chapter 3
- Day 4: Pg.42-Top of Pg.52
- Day 5: Pg.52-Pg.58

Related Picture Books:

- *A New Nation: The United States: 1783-1815* by Betsy Maestro

Possible Reader:

- *Wagon Train*, Kramer

Optional Copywork: Abigail Adams cared deeply about her country.

Activity: Spoon Doll

In Colonial days, most boys and girls did not have toys that came from stores. They had to be creative, so they made their own toys and dolls. Even a wooden spoon can be made into a simple doll.

Materials:
-Any size wooden spoon (or two to make a pair of dolls)
-Permanent markers, or acrylic paints and a fine tip paint brush
*Optional: yarn for hair, scraps of fabric for clothes, craft glue

•This activity can be as simple or as involved as you choose to make it! Your student can just add facial features to the spoon using different colors, and then color the handle as they desire (could add a column of buttons, etc).

•You can also use craft glue to attach small bits of colored yarn as hair. If you have scraps of fabric, cut out a dress or shirt and pants (making a front and a back piece of each). Then, spread craft glue along the front and back of the spoon handle, and on the insides of the clothes. Press the clothes onto the handle, also pressing the front and back sides together.

•Give your spoon doll a name and have fun playing!

Notes

Abigail Adams, Part 1

A long time ago, many things in America were very different than how they are today. At the time when the Founding Fathers wrote the Constitution, only men were allowed to help make laws. Women had the important work of taking care of their homes and bringing up children. However, women also played a role in forming the new government. Many supported their husbands and shared their own ideas. One of these women was Abigail Adams.

When she was born, her name was Abigail Smith. Her father was a minister in a church, and her mother worked very hard to teach her children at home. Although little brown haired Abigail never went to school, she learned to read and write from her father and mother. Their small home did not have very many fancy things in it, but it did have lots and lots of books! There were books on almost every subject Abigail could imagine. Philosophy, theology, classics, plays, history, government and law books lined the shelves of her father's library. When her father was home in the evenings, his five children would happily sit around him and listen to him read from these books. With the flames gently flickering in the fireplace and the soothing voice of their father reading, the children felt peaceful and content. There were many big, long words in the books that they did not quite understand, but Father would pause now and then to explain what he had been reading to them. Abigail was often sick as a little girl, but she continued to read those books as she rested in her bed. Over the years, Abigail became very knowledgeable about all those subjects. She was very thankful, because she knew that most other little girls were never taught the way she was.

When Abigail was nineteen years old, she married a man named John Adams. He was a lawyer, and a very smart man. Standing in the parlor of Abigail's home, her own father performed the wedding. Once the simple ceremony was over, the young couple drove a horse and carriage a few miles away to their first little home. John and Abigail ended up moving to other houses throughout their lives, but wherever they lived, Abigail worked hard to make it home. She had their first baby soon after their marriage, and before long four more followed! Besides taking care of her children, she was very busy growing food for their family in her garden, cleaning the home and sewing clothes for all of them. Her husband was usually not there to help, because he was one of the men helping to write the Declaration of Independence! After that, he had to travel to Europe for a long time.

Throughout all the months and years that John and Abigail Adams spent apart, they wrote more than a thousand letters back and forth to one another. Sometimes John wrote two letters in one day to his wife! These letters were full of talk about the children, their farm, how they missed each other. They were also full of discussion about government and what laws should be made for the new nation. Abigail had many good ideas that she shared with her husband. She reminded him not to forget about the rights of women, who needed education as much as men did. She said that educated mothers would be able to raise educated children. Her faithful support and her ideas helped her husband greatly!

Review Questions:

1. How did Abigail learn to read and write when she was young?
2. What was one way Abigail Adams was able to help her husband?

Abigail Adams, Part 2

During her husband's absences, Abigail Adams was very busy. John had left the farm in her capable hands. She oversaw the planting of crops, hiring help, and caring for the livestock. Not only did she have all the work that an ordinary wife and mother had in those days, but she also did the work of her husband, too! She once said that she hoped to be as good of a farmer as her husband was as a lawyer. From sunup to sundown she cooked for her children, nursed their illnesses, taught them to read and write, sewed clothes, milked cows, fed chickens, weeded gardens, wrote letters to her husband and much more. One would think that with so many things to do every day, Abigail Adams surely did not have time for anything outside of her own family. But she did!

Abigail Adams cared deeply about her country. She wanted to do everything she could to help America win the war for independence. She felt very strongly that the words of the Declaration of Independence were true: that every man was created equal, and that every person was born with rights. She believed that women were created equal, too, and that their rights should be protected. She wrote about all of her feelings to her husband, urging him to remember what they were fighting for.

During the war, soldiers heard about the kindness and patriotism of Abigail Adams. It became known everywhere that her house was always open to her countrymen. Day after day, and even during the nights, soldiers would show up at her door. Sometimes they were hungry, and Abigail would give them all the food they needed. Sometimes they were cold and wet, and Abigail would let them rest in her home and warm themselves by her fire. Sometimes they were ill or wounded, and Abigail would nurse them as she nursed her own children. It did not matter that this made more work for her to do. She knew that these men were risking their lives fighting for the same things that she believed in, and she wanted to do all she could to help. John and Abigail both felt relief and joy once the war was finished and America had become a free country. They had served their country well, but there was still more in store for the Adams!

When George Washington was made president, John Adams became the Vice President. Being Vice President was an important job. Not only did John Adams help George Washington make big decisions about how things should be done in the United States, but he was also ready to become the president in case anything should happen to George Washington. Finally, once George Washington decided not to be president again after his first two terms, who do you think was elected as the second president of the United States? John Adams! Abigail became the First Lady, which is what we call the wife of the president. Together they moved to the nation's new capitol: Washington D.C. They were the first people to ever live in the White House, which is where all of America's presidents have lived ever since!

Review Questions:

1. What were some of the ways Abigail Adams helped serve her country?
2. Who became the second president of the United States?

Adventures in America Week 21

	Day 1	Day 2	Day 3
Reading	Read *Francis Scott Key*	Read *Star Spangled Banner*	Read *Smart About* pg.22 and 56
Coloring/ Activity	Coloring Page, pg. 99	"Watercolor Flag" activity	Color Iowa and Wisconsin on blank US map, pg. 2
Notebook	Narration from Read Aloud, history or reader, pg. 100	Copywork, pg. 101	Fill out notebook page for Iowa and Wisconsin, pgs. 102, 103

Optional Read-Aloud:

The Cabin Faced West
- Day 1: Chapter 5
- Day 2: Chapter 6
- Day 3: Chapter 7
- Day 4: Pg.102-Bottom of Pg.112
- Day 5: Pg.112-Pg.122, plus postscript

Related Picture Books:

- *The Star Spangled Banner*, illus. by Ingri & Edgar Parin D'Aulaire

Possible Reader:

- *Long Way to a New Land*, Sandin

Activity: Watercolor Flag
Materials:
- Sheet of white paper
- Red and blue watercolor paint
- Ruler, pencil
- White crayon
- Paintbrushes
- Masking tape

• Use a ruler to pencil lines for the stripes and outline the corner for the stars.

• Let your student use a white crayon and draw lots of stars in the top left corner. If he cannot draw stars, try using 3 small lines that intersect in the middle (think asterisk *). Press down with crayon!

• Place masking tape on the edges of every other stripe, covering up what will be left white, and leaving the others exposed (to be red).

• Use red watercolor to fill in the empty stripes. Immediately, gently lift off masking tape to expose white stripes.

• Using blue watercolor, paint over the top left corner. The white crayon marks will show up through the paint. Let dry.

Optional Copywork: As the haze began to lift, the flag could be seen clearly.

Note Try to have an American flag on hand to look at while reading Day 2 *Star Spangled Banner*. *Smart About the Fifty States* also has some pictures of how the flag has changed on pg. 59.

Notes

Francis Scott Key

Years and years after America had won the war with England, there were still problems between the two countries. Finally, there was another war! This time the war would end quickly, and America and England would end up as better friends than ever. One very special song was written during this war. It is called the "Star Spangled Banner," and it is our national anthem. You may have heard it sung before a sports event. Normally, Americans stand up and look at the American flag while it is being sung. To show honor to the flag, many people place their right hand over their heart during the song. It is a very special song to Americans! A man named Francis Scott Key wrote the words.

Francis Scott Key was a lawyer, but he was also a poet. Poets write verses about the world, the things they see or the way they feel. Francis Scott Key was in Baltimore during the War of 1812, which was America's second war with England. One day, he learned that his good friend Dr. Beanes had been taken prisoner by the British! He felt fearful and worried for his friend. He knew he had to do something to help! He anxiously asked the president for help in setting his friend free. A man named John Skinner came to help him.

Together, Francis Scott Key and John Skinner negotiated with the British general. They enjoyed a nice dinner together on a boat in the water just outside of Baltimore. The British general agreed that Dr. Beanes would be released to go with them, but said that first they must stay on board for awhile. The British had plans to attack Fort McHenry in Baltimore, and they did not want Francis Scott Key or the other men to go free until the attack was finished. Sadly, the three men were forced to simply watch and wait while their countrymen were under fire.

Night fell over both the water and the land. It was not all dark, though. Bursts of light shone now and then as bombs exploded in the distance. With gunshots ringing out all around them, the three Americans gazed on in despair. Suddenly they saw something waving high in the air over the fort. What was that? It was the flag, and it was waving proudly. The men anxiously watched, wondering whether that flag was a flag of England or their own beloved Stars and Stripes. Straining their eyes in the darkness, they watched and watched. Finally, glimmers of dawn lightened their surroundings. A smoky haze from the guns and cannons lingered over the land. As the haze began to lift, the flag could be seen clearly. No, it was not the dreaded English flag that was raised over Fort McHenry. It was indeed the Stars and Stripes of the United States! She was certainly distressed from the battle, and was torn by cannon balls that had flown right through her. But she still flew proud and glorious over the land of the free!

Francis Scott Key felt his heart pound with emotion as he looked over at the American flag. Overcome by the love he felt for his country, he took a letter from his pocket. Turning it over, he wrote a poem on the back of the paper. The poem began like this: (See Page 143)

These words were set to music and people began to listen to the song all over America. Soon, it was chosen to be the national anthem of the United States. Now, whenever any American hears the Star Spangled Banner sung, they are reminded of the glorious sight of her flag waving proud and strong in the midst of battle.

Review Questions:

1. Where was Francis Scott Key as he watched the attack on Fort McHenry?
2. What sight led Francis Scott Key to write the words to the Star Spangled Banner?

The Star Spangled Banner

When Francis Scott Key looked out from where he stood on the boat, it was no wonder that he could see the flag waving above Fort McHenry. The flag was much larger than most flags that we see displayed. It was actually thirty feet tall and forty-two feet long! That is bigger than many living rooms. A woman name Mary Pickersgill had been asked to sew the flag for Fort McHenry. Mary Pickersgill was used to making signal flags for ships. This flag would be much larger than any she had ever made. She asked her thirteen year old daughter and two young nieces to help her with the job of sewing. First they made smaller strips of red, white and blue cloth. Then, they stitched those strips together until the stripes were nice and big. Day after day, and week after week the ladies labored together making the flag. It was an important job, and they wanted to do their very best. Finally, after seven long weeks of careful sewing, the flag was completed! Mary Pickersgill had no idea that the same large flag would soon mark the spot of a historic battle, and become the inspiration for one of the country's most well known songs!

Since the first five pointed star made by Betsy Ross, the American flag has gone through many changes. Each part of the flag has a meaning behind it. If you count all of the stripes, you will see that there are thirteen all together. That is because the United States of America began as just thirteen colonies! Those colonies became states, and over time more and more states were added to the nation. Instead of adding more stripes onto the flag, a star was added for every state. If you take the time to count all of the stars on the flag today, you will find that there are fifty. How many states do you think there are now? There are fifty, one for every star!

The symbols and colors on the flag all have meanings, too. Stars were chosen because they are a symbol of the heavens. The stripes are symbols of rays of light coming out from the sun. Seven of the stripes are red, which stands for courage. The six white stripes symbolize purity. The blue background behind the stars stands for justice. Although the flag today shows the stars lined up in rows, the first flag had the stars in a circle. George Washington wanted to show that no state was more important than another. He also said that the stars on the flag were similar to a new constellation for the heavens, just as America was a new kind of nation on earth.

Today the American flag is just as important as ever. It has many special rules about how it is to be displayed, handled and stored. For example, when the flag is being lowered, it should never touch the ground. It should always be folded neatly and stored carefully. On holidays, the flag is raised to full mast, which means that it is all the way up to the top of the flag pole. On days of sadness and mourning, the flag is only raised half-mast, which means that it is only half way up the flag pole. In many schools and other places, people pledge allegiance to the flag every day. This is usually done standing up, with the right hand held over the heart. The words go like this:

I pledge allegiance to the Flag
Of the United States of America,
And to the Republic for which it stands,
One Nation under God,
Indivisible, with Liberty and Justice for all.

Review Questions:

1. Who made the large flag that was flying over Fort McHenry?
2. How many stars and stripes are on the American flag?

Adventures in America Week 22

	Day 1	Day 2	Day 3
Reading	Read *Lewis and Clark's Expedition*	Read *Lewis and Clark Journey On*	Read *Smart About* pg.12
Coloring/ Activity	Coloring Page, pg. 105	"Binoculars" activity	Color California on blank US map, pg. 2
Notebook	Narration from Read Aloud, history or reader, pg. 106	Copywork, pg. 107	Fill out notebook page for California, pg. 108

Optional Read-Aloud:

Little House on the Prairie
- Day 1: Chapter 1
- Day 2: Chapter 2
- Day 3: Chapter 3
- Day 4: Chapter 4
- Day 5: Chapter 5

Related Picture Books:

- *How We Crossed the West*, by Rosalyn Schanzer

Possible Reader:

- *Long Way to a New Land*, Sandin

Activity: Binoculars

Materials:
- Two empty toilet paper rolls
- Ribbon or yarn
- Construction paper
- Scissors

• Cut a sheet of construction paper so that it is the same length as the toilet paper rolls. Holding the two rolls together side by side, wrap the construction paper around them and secure with tape.

• Tape a long piece of ribbon or yarn to outsides of the binoculars for wearing around student's neck.

• Take outside if weather permits, and have fun exploring!

Optional Copywork: Merriweather Lewis and William Clark were soldiers who had the courage that such a dangerous expedition would demand.

Notes

Lewis and Clark's Expedition

Up until now most Americans lived in the East, where the first settlers had arrived and where the big cities were. Farther west the land stretched on in an amazing wilderness of uninhabited forests, prairies full of buffalo, scorching deserts and majestic mountains. These lands were home to many different Native American nations who knew how to survive off the wildlife in each place. By now there was a third president living in the White House. It was Thomas Jefferson, the man who had written most of the Declaration of Independence. Soon President Jefferson decided that Americans had better take it upon themselves to explore these mysterious lands all the way to the Pacific Ocean. If America did not claim the land for trade herself, another country may take it first! It would also be a wonderful opportunity to study new plants and animals, and to make friends with the native tribes.

President Jefferson found two men who knew how to navigate a river and how to collect scientific data. Merriweather Lewis and William Clark were soldiers who had the courage that such a dangerous expedition would demand. They prepared three boats that they planned to sail along the Missouri River, all the way from St. Louis to the Pacific Ocean. No one had ever done this before, but they suspected that it could be done. A river route from the east to the west coast was called the Northwest Passage, and it was this passage that Lewis and Clark aimed to find. They loaded the boats full of scientific equipment that would help them do experiments along the way. They also packed gifts for the Native Americans, flags, medicine and Indian Peace Medals. These silver medals had a portrait of President Jefferson on them and would be handed out to the tribes they would meet. Hopefully, the medals would show the Indians that they wanted peace with them. Having peace was very important for at least two reasons. One, they did not want to be attacked or have to fight on their journey. Two, they wanted to be able to trade with the Indians for food and supplies they would need. If they became friends now, other Americans would also be able to trade with the Indians in the future. They hoped for peace, but they also brought along powerful weapons so that they could display strong military firepower if needed.

Finally the day arrived when all their preparations were finished. Forty-five men sailed out together. They waved good-bye to the crowds of people and watched as civilization slowly faded from sight. Soon the buildings disappeared except for a lone cabin or two, or once in a while a tiny village. Before long, they were completely surrounded by wilderness, in a land that no one had ever charted. There was no map to show them what lie ahead beyond the curve of the river. They did not know what kinds of wild animals might be prowling on the shores. They did not even know how long it would take them to arrive at the other end of their journey. What kinds of Indians lived in those hills? Was there any food to eat once they had passed the prairies? Could they possibly survive? All they had were questions, but they were determined to discover all the answers.

Review Questions:

1. What were Lewis and Clark trying to find?
2. Why was it important to have peace with the Indians?

Lewis and Clark Journey On

"Grrrrrrr!" came the low rumble of a roar from the shores. The men on the boat watched, wide eyed. They had seen huge elk before that stood taller than a man and boasted powerful antlers. They had seen small black bears that lived in the mountains and forests in the East. They had been awestruck at the sight of herds of buffalo a thousand strong, lumbering across the vast prairies and grazing on the tall grasses and brush. But their eyes had never witnessed this ferocious looking beast. The huge animal rose up so that it was standing on its two back legs! Its head was so high that it must be twice as tall as a man! It roared again, and then splashed into the water. Swiftly its paw reached down into the shallow waves and rose up again, this time with a shiny, silver fish wriggling in its grasp.

The animal was a grizzly bear, one of the most impressive and dangerous mammals of North America. It was just one of many new animals that had never before been documented by science. As part of their search for the Northwest Passage, Lewis and Clark were also performing scientific experiments on the soil, plant-life and animals that they discovered along the way. While Clark spent most of his time on the boat, carefully charting out their course and drawing detailed maps of each new section of river, Lewis much preferred to be on the shores, peering through his magnifying glass at new specimens. He collected samples of dirt and rocks, and made collections of bugs and plants. He carefully drew pictures of the various birds and animals that they found. Besides the grizzly bear, they discovered hundreds of other new wildlife, such as the Canada goose, coyote, Habor seal, mountain lion, red fox, striped skunk, mountain goat and bull snake. Lewis even took a prairie dog to be sent back as a gift for President Thomas Jefferson.

As the days passed by, the air turned colder, and the men knew that they would need to find a safe place to stay for the winter. They built a little settlement called Fort Mandan, in today's North Dakota. They probably would have starved if they hadn't received food and help from some nearby friendly Indians. One of the Indians, Sacagawea, would end up assisting them in many ways on the journey ahead. Eventually the snow melted away and they could continue their expedition.

Since they were not really sure where the Northwest Passage would be found, the men split up to follow different branches of the river. One of the groups climbed a hill and looked over the other side. They almost could not believe their eyes when they saw the ocean! Blue water that sparkled and stretched out as far as they could see! They had made it all the way to the Pacific, but they had not found a Northwest Passage where their boats could sail all the way through the land. Still, they had arrived at their destination and made many important discoveries along the way. They returned home, where President Jefferson and others gratefully received their hundreds of carefully drawn maps, souvenirs from friendly Indian tribes and descriptions of newly discovered wildlife.

Although they did not find a Northwest Passage, Lewis and Clark's expedition was very important in America's history. Because of their discoveries, the land from coast to coast was claimed for trade by America and not another European country. The Indians began to trade more and more with Americans. Every year, more settlers would venture out farther west, using the maps and other helpful information that Lewis and Clark had gathered. Their bravery and careful, hard work opened the way for a nation to grow westward.

Review Questions:

1. What were some of the animals Lewis and Clark discovered on their expedition?
2. Why was their expedition important?

Adventures in America Week 23

	Day 1	Day 2	Day 3
Reading	Read *Sacagawea, Part 1*	Read *Sacagawea, Part 2*	Read *Smart About* pg.30 and 44
Coloring/ Activity	Coloring Page, pg. 109	"Buffalo Hide Map" activity	Color Minnesota and Oregon on blank US map, pg. 2
Notebook	Narration from Read Aloud, history or reader, pg. 110	Copywork, pg. 111	Fill out notebook page for Minnesota and Oregon, pgs. 112, 113

Optional Read-Aloud:

Little House on the Prairie
- Day 1: Chapter 6
- Day 2: Chapter 7
- Day 3: Chapter 8
- Day 4: Chapter 9
- Day 5: Chapter 10

Related Picture Books:

- *Sacagawea,* by Liselotte Erdrich

Possible Reader:

- *Lewis and Clark: A Prairie Dog for the President*, Redmond

Activity: Buffalo Hide Map

After a successful hunt, the Shoshone Indians would draw a map or a picture of what had taken place. This was a way to memorialize the men's bravery and their gratitude for the meat provided.

Materials:
-Brown paper grocery bag   -Scissors
-One or two dark color markers

•Cut bag open. Tear around the edges.

•Crumple bag and reopen, laying flat.

•Use markers to draw simple figures depicting a buffalo hunt. You may want to offer examples of how to simplistically draw a buffalo and men, and give a suggestion of what the hunt may have looked like. (For example, there was a large group of buffalo up ahead near a cliff, the men rode on horses surrounding them and used bows and arrows to shoot the buffalo. Six of the buffalo fell.)

Optional Copywork: Sacagawea was the daughter of a great Shoshone chief.

Notes

Sacagawea, Part 1

About fifteen years before Lewis and Clark set out on their great expedition, a little girl was born in one of the areas they would eventually travel through. Sacagawea was the daughter of a great Shoshone chief. The Shoshone Indians lived in teepees and ate the meat from the buffalo they hunted. Life was difficult for them, and the people had to be strong and brave to survive. Their long time enemies, the Hidatsa, were nearby. For years and years, there had been skirmishes between the Hidatsa and the Shoshone tribes. On both sides, the warriors fought courageously. Sometimes one group would emerge victorious, and other times the others would be the conquerors. At the time of Sacagawea's birth, the Hidatsa were strong and mighty compared to the Shoshone. When Sacagawea was twelve years old, she and a group of friends were captured by the Hidatsa and taken as their prisoners.

The young girl was probably very frightened, but she knew she had to be brave no matter what happened to her. She lived in the Hidatsa village for several years. When she was fifteen, a white man came near the village. His name was Toussaint Charbonneau. He was French-Canadian, and a fur-trader. He trapped and hunted animals in the wilderness and sold the furs for money or goods. Sacagawea was sold to this man, and became his wife. They lived together among the Hidatsa and Mandan Indians. Before long, more white men appeared on the land.

This time it was Lewis and Clark's expedition that had arrived, seeking shelter for the cold winter. William Clark met Charbonneau and knew it would be helpful to have somebody who could speak the local languages. He immediately tried to hire Charbonneau as an interpreter. An interpreter had a very special job on journeys like this one. By understanding different languages, he could help the men get along with the Indians they would meet. Without sharing language, it was very difficult for white men and Indians to understand each other's strange ways. With an interpreter, hopefully they could trade peacefully and avoid fighting. Once William Clark learned that Charbonneau also had a Shoshone wife, he was anxious that Sacagawea should accompany the men as well. He had heard that the Shoshone had horses. When the group reached the Rocky Mountains, they would need horses to carry their equipment and supplies over the mountain passes. Would the Shoshone be willing to trade their horses? Surely if they brought Sacagawea along, the Shoshone would want to help them.

Not only was Sacagawea a woman and very young, she was also expecting a child. Including a young mother and a newborn infant on the expedition could be challenging. Merriweather Lewis and William Clark discussed whether to bring her, and concluded that having a mother and child along might make the group seem less threatening. Charbonneau agreed to take his wife, and the matter was settled. Once the cold winter was over, the group would continue their journey to find the Northwest Passage. The men hoped that hiring Charbonneau and his Shoshone wife would prove to be a wise decision.

Review Questions:

1. What happened to Sacagawea as a young girl?
2. Why did Lewis and Clark want to hire Charbonneau and Sacagawea to travel with them?

Sacagawea, Part 2

During the winter, the men in Lewis and Clark's expedition huddled under blankets to stay warm inside their Mandan Fort. With a thick layer of snow covering the ground and all the animals staying in their cozy homes, the men soon grew hungry. There did not appear to be anything to eat in this frozen land. Thankfully, the friendly Hidatsa and Mandan Indians offered to help the men survive the winter. They brought their own food to share and to trade with the white men. Without this kindness, the men may not have lasted through the harsh North Dakota winter.

Merriweather Lewis offered his help to the Indians as well. He was the doctor of the expedition, and had carried along a supply of medicines for various illnesses. On several occasions, he was able to help a sick or injured Indian. One night in February, he was called on to help the young Sacagawea give birth to her baby. Sacagawea had been waiting a very long time and was worn and tired. One man advised Captain Lewis to give her a small portion of the rattle from a rattlesnake to help her baby come. Captain Lewis did have some bits of a rattle and decided he would follow the strange advice and see what happened. He mixed it with water and gave some to Sacagawea to drink. Within ten minutes, a strong baby boy had been born! He was named Jean Baptiste.

Soon the winter snows melted and spring was upon them. It was time for the expedition to journey forth, including the French Canadian fur trader Charbonneau, the young Shoshone woman Sacagawea and the newborn baby boy Jean Baptiste. It was no time at all before the captains realized how valuable Sacagawea was to them. She knew how to find plants, herbs and roots that could be eaten or used as medicine to keep them all healthy. She was patient and hardworking throughout their travels, even while carrying her son the whole way. One time the canoe she was in capsized, spilling its boxes of precious materials and important papers into the river. Acting quickly, Sacagawea was able to rescue the important items.

As the expedition reached Shoshone territory, they soon found the leader of a local tribe. This would be just the man to ask for the horses they would need for crossing the Rocky Mountains! But would he be willing to talk with them? They invited him inside their tent and called for Sacagawea to come translate the language. Sacagawea began to interpret and then looked more closely at the Shoshone man. All of a sudden, she jumped to her feet and crossed the tent, throwing her arms around him and weeping loudly. It was her own brother, whom she had not laid eyes on since her capture as a young girl! The brother and sister embraced joyfully before the meeting continued. Of course he was willing to help! He happily gave them the horses they needed.

Over and over again, Sacagawea proved her worth to the expedition. The men would never forget the important role she had played in helping them survive and find their way. Years after the journey, Sacagawea had a baby girl and later died. Captain William Clark took care of her two children, always remembering the courage their mother had shown.

Review Questions:

1. How did Sacagawea help the expedition?
2. Who did Sacagawea unexpectedly meet along the way?

Adventures in America Week 24

	Day 1	**Day 2**	**Day 3**
Reading	Read *Traveling the Oregon Trail, Part 1*	Read *Traveling the Oregon Trail, Part 2*	Read *Smart About* pg.23
Coloring/ Activity	Coloring Page, pg. 115	"Covered Wagon" activity	Color Kansas on blank US map, pg. 2
Notebook	Narration from Read Aloud, history or reader, pg. 116	Copywork, pg. 117	Fill out notebook page for Kansas, pg. 118

Optional Read-Aloud:

Little House on the Prairie
- Day 1: Chapter 11
- Day 2: Chapter 12
- Day 3: Chapter 13
- Day 4: Chapter 14
- Day 5: Chapter 15

Related Picture Books:

- *Daily Life in a Covered Wagon,* by Paul Erickson

Possible Reader:

- *Lewis and Clark: A Prairie Dog for the President,* Redmond

Optional Copywork: The covered wagons traveled about fifteen miles every day along the Oregon Trail.

Activity: Covered Wagon
Materials:
-Pint size milk carton, empty and clean   -Craft glue
-White and brown construction paper
-4 black circles cut from cardstock (or cardboard circles painted black)

•Cut milk carton in half from top to bottom.

•Cover bottom of carton with brown paper, or your student could paint it brown. If using paint, adding a bit of glue to the paint first will help it better adhere to the carton.

•Lay carton on side and attach a piece of white paper in an arch over the top with tape or glue. Let the tapered part of the carton stick out in front a bit.

•Glue the black circles onto the bottom of the carton, one side at a time. Place them so they are mostly attached to the carton with a small amount hanging over the edge, to resemble wheels.

•Once dry, you can use toy people and livestock to act out what it was like traveling on the Oregon Trail!

Notes

Traveling the Oregon Trail, Part 1

In the years after Lewis and Clark first explored the western lands along the Missouri River, more and more people wanted to settle there. The East was becoming increasingly crowded as ships full of people emigrated from other countries and as families grew. It was common for families to have six, seven, eight or even more children. As these children grew up and started their own families, the land became scarce. Many men wanted to farm, but there just was not much land available anymore. So, they turned their eyes westward.

There was a beautiful dream of vast, fertile lands watered by crystal clear springs and flowing rivers. Woods and prairies that were still teeming with game tempted skilled hunters. An overland route had been discovered. This trail wiggled along for two thousand miles and connected towns along the Missouri River all the way to Oregon, on the west coast. At first the trails were only passable on a horse or on foot, but men worked hard to clear the way so that wagons could travel on them.

It was spring and Emma and Henry were standing out of the way, watching the men load the wagon. Their family would join about fifty other families, all eager to travel west on what was now named the Oregon Trail. Their wagons would line up in what was called a wagon train. By traveling together as a large group, they would be able to help each other. Along the way, they may have to build bridges to cross small rivers, give medical care to those who would fall ill, and help to find and prepare food to eat. They would be on the trail for about six months and would hopefully reach a new home before the freezing winter snows came.

Henry watched his pa hook up the six oxen to the front of their covered wagon. The oxen were sturdy and strong. They would be able to pull the heavy load day after day. Pa had worked hard to train them before they left. Now they could obey his commands of "Gee," which meant turn to the right, and "Haw," meaning to the left. Pa had explained that there would be time and opportunity enough once they reached Oregon to buy fresh horses, but now he wanted reliable beasts of burden that wouldn't stray off when they camped for the night.

Inside the wagon, Emma could hardly turn around, filled as it was with barrels and crates full of the food they would need on the trail. The men said there might be good hunting along the way which would provide fresh meat, but then again, there might not. Besides, they would have to use almost all the daylight hours for moving on ahead and there would not be much time to look around for food. Emma's mother had carefully kept a list of all the recommended food supplies a family should bring. There were hundreds of pounds of flour, cornmeal, bacon, sugar, coffee, dried fruit, salt, rice and beans. It was all stored away into water-tight barrels so that it would not spoil before they reached Oregon. Looking at the impressive mountain of goods, Emma could hardly believe her family could possibly eat so much in six months! Besides the edible provisions, there were also crates loaded with kettles, knives and spoons for cooking. Quilts that Mother and Aunty had worked on over the last year were neatly folded in bundles along with two changes of clothing for each person and three pillows. Emma tightened her black leather boots. There were many additional pairs of boots in the wagon, since they would each wear out two to three pairs walking along the trail. Before she knew it, Pa was saying it was finally time to begin their travels!

Review Questions:

1. Why did people travel together in wagon trains on the Oregon Trail?
2. What kinds of provisions did travelers bring with them?

Traveling the Oregon Trail, Part 2

Henry and Emma sat around their family's campfire, quietly munching on a biscuit. For three months now they had eaten almost nothing but bacon, beans and biscuits for every meal. They dearly missed having fresh eggs for breakfast or a bit of cheese with their lunch. As soon as they arrived in Oregon they would build themselves a proper home and garden, and then they could grow their own food again.

Henry stood up, stretched, and looked ahead. He guessed they would move on shortly, since the sun was up now. Yesterday had been Sunday, the only day of the week they did not travel. It had provided a much needed rest for not only the animals, but for the weary feet of all the travelers as well. Riding inside the wagon was just too bumpy and dusty for comfort. He and Emma usually ended up walking instead. They journeyed about fifteen miles every day, and the children were getting used to the exercise. By now they quite enjoyed the chance to walk side by side with their new friends. It was also fun to look around at the changes in the land as they went farther and farther west.

Henry knew that they had it pretty easy so far compared to some other wagon trains. There were rumors of another train that had set out just two weeks before their own but had run into devastating trouble. As they had moved farther west, they found that winter still lingered there. The grass had just not begun to grow enough to sustain their animals, and many of the oxen and mules had starved in the barren land. Without enough animals left to pull the heavy wagons, the people had to abandon many of their carefully packed goods. Crates full of tools, coffee, or books were left on the side of the road for future travelers to find. It was always a bit exciting to see the boxes up ahead and wonder whether they might contain some desperately needed item. Another wagon train last year had been infected by the terrible disease of cholera. Once it had started, the disease spread throughout the camp and claimed the lives of many. Other wagons had nearly reached their destination only to find that winter had fallen early and the mountain passes were too covered with snow to safely pass. Henry felt thankful that their own wagon train had enjoyed good health and abundant grass for the oxen.

Life on the trail was beginning to feel almost normal to these pioneers. They had settled into a comfortable routine of walking every day except Sunday. The womenfolk enjoyed telling stories and sharing advice as they walked. They looked out for each other's children, and there was rarely any mischief a little one could get into with so many eyes on him or her! Once a month or so they made good use of a river and washed their family's clothes, which had all faded to a nondescript brown from constant exposure to the sun and dust from the trail. In the evenings around their campfires, they pulled out their pins, scissors, needles and thread and went to work patching holes in pants or darning socks, while the men would sometimes read from the Bible or play the fiddle and sing. They all made the most of the difficult circumstances and dreamed of the new homes they would soon build. It took lots of courage to venture out into the unknown with a family in tow. These men and women knew that great risks lay ahead of them, and yet they held firmly to their dreams and set about doing the hard work that was required of them.

Review Questions:

1. What did a typical meal consist of on the Oregon Trail?
2. What were some hardships the travelers faced?

Adventures in America Week 25

	Day 1	Day 2	Day 3
Reading	Read *Pioneer Days, Part 1*	Read *Pioneer Days, Part 2*	Read *Smart About* pg.55
Coloring/ Activity	Coloring Page, pg. 119	"Oiled Paper Windows" activity	Color West Virginia on blank US map, pg. 2
Notebook	Narration from Read Aloud, history or reader, pg. 120	Copywork, pg. 121	Fill out notebook page for West Virginia, pg. 122

Optional Read-Aloud:

Little House on the Prairie
- Day 1: Chapter 16
- Day 2: Chapter 17
- Day 3: Chapter 18
- Day 4: Chapter 19
- Day 5: Chapter 20

Related Picture Books:
- *Ox-Cart Man,* by Donald Hall

Possible Reader:
- *Long Way Westward,* Sandin

Activity: Oiled Paper Window

Before many people could afford glass window panes, oiled paper was another way to still let some sunlight come into a log cabin.

Materials:
-Sheet of white paper   -Cotton ball
-Vegetable oil (any kind of cooking oil should work fine)

•Dab the cotton ball into a small amount of vegetable oil.

•Spread it all over one side of the paper. Let dry.

•Turn paper over, and spread oil on the other side. Let dry.

•Place your oiled paper up to a window and watch how the light shines through! You could also hold up an un-oiled sheet of paper to see the difference.

Optional Copywork: Living on the prairie required lots of hard work from everyone.

Notes

Pioneer Days, Part 1

Ma opened her eyes and rolled over in her bed. Pa was just sitting up and lighting the small grease lamp that sat on the shelf next to him. Soon, the scent of the greasy black smoke crept into the air of the room. Ma pulled the quilt tightly over her head, blocking out the smell and hoping for just a moment more of sleep. "Wah!" came the cry from the cradle next to her. Sleep would have to wait until tonight, Ma thought to herself.

She lifted baby Timothy from the wooden cradle that Pa had built last summer. It had a special hood over the head that would keep the cold winter winds from bothering him in the months to come. While Pa pulled on his boots and headed outside to the barn to milk the cows and feed the pigs and chickens, Ma hurried to light the fire in the wood stove. Once that was done, the cabin felt warm and cozy. Now there was also light to see by. Not much sunlight streamed through their small oiled paper window. Someday they would have enough money to buy real glass window panes. She heated some water for the family to use for washing their faces and hands. After feeding Timothy and laying him back in his cradle, she mixed dough for the day's biscuits. By the time they were finishing baking, she could hear the children stirring in the loft upstairs.

Indeed, at that moment Sarah, Wade and Albert were getting dressed. It was a simple task because they each had only two sets of clothes to choose from. One dress or shirt and pants for school days, and one fancier set for Sundays or holidays. Since today was a school day, they each put on their ordinary clothes and climbed down the ladder just as Pa entered the door with a full pail of milk. Sarah took the pail and poured its contents into the milk pan. The milk pan was a shallow dish with edges that turned out at the top. Milk sat in the pan until the cream separated and could be skimmed from the top with a spoon. One of Sarah's chores was skimming the cream and making homemade butter with it.

After they had finished their breakfast, the children took their lard pails which Ma had filled with more biscuits, an apple and a small piece of cold pork. This would be their lunch that they would eat at school. Some of the students lived in the town and could walk home for the midday meal, but the Humphreys lived in the country. It was quite a hike for the kids to walk the two miles to and from school, so they carried their lunches with them.

With the cabin mostly empty, Ma hurried to complete her housework during Timothy's nap. She climbed the ladder to the loft and retrieved the full chamber pots from under the beds. These would have to be taken to the outhouse and cleaned out there. After that task was finished, she moved a pot of soup to the stove where it could slowly simmer until it was time for lunch. Next, she stepped outside into the garden to weed around her precious vegetables, roots and herbs. Buying these kinds of food in the town was simply too expensive, and the only way her family could afford to eat them was if Ma grew them herself. It was one of her favorite chores of the day. As she worked, she thought about how blessed their family was to have successfully made a home here on the Western frontier. They were all healthy and happy. Ma hummed contentedly as she tugged at the weeds.

Review Questions:

1. How many sets of clothes did the Humphrey children have?
2. What kind of windows did the Humphrey's home have?

Pioneer Days, Part 2

Once the gardening had been finished for the day, Ma headed inside the cabin to make bread. She added flour, salt and water to her starter dough in the bread trough. The bread trough looked like a miniature baby cradle and sat on top of her table. It was the perfect place for kneading dough, letting it rise, and keeping the starter dough that she set aside from every batch. The starter was full of yeast, which made the bread rise nice and high and gave it a delicious flavor once baked.

Whether working out in the fields and barn, or in the garden and house, living on the prairie required lots of hard work from everyone. Even the children did their share to help around the house. Once they arrived home from school, they hurried to finish their chores. If the chores and homework were completed early, they would still have some daylight for playing before bedtime. Wade skipped down the hill to the spring. Coming back up was much harder, since he was carrying two heavy pails filled to the brim with fresh spring water. He tried to keep them steady and not let the water splash out as he stumbled up the steep hill. While Wade struggled with the water pails, Albert went out to the wood pile to fetch wood for the stove. He gathered a neat bundle together and brought it inside the cabin. Sarah was busy churning the day's fresh cream into butter. Albert's mouth watered as he thought of the tasty johnnycakes and fresh butter they would soon have. Once their chores were completed, they sat at the table and did their homework. They took turns finding the pages they needed in the spelling book that they all shared. Like most families, the Humphreys could only afford to buy one book for all the children to use.

Soon supper was spread out on the table and the children gathered around, with Pa and Ma seated at the ends. There was roast pork, boiled potatoes from the garden and the johnnycakes and butter that they had all been anticipating. With bowed heads, they thanked the Lord who had taken care of their family and given them this food to eat. During the meal, they all shared about the day at school and home.

Wade excitedly informed his parents that his paper had been chosen as the winner in the school essay contest. Next week, there would be a special presentation before all the students and parents and he would stand up and read what he had written. He beamed with pride as Pa grinned and congratulated him. The whole school was taught together in one room, including students from six years old all the way to fourteen years old. Since Wade was only twelve, his essay had been chosen over some of the older children's. Wade loved to write and had even composed several poems. His family only owned three books which were the Bible, the Almanac and a family doctor book. Wade dreamed of one day writing a book on his own. Then, his parents and sister and brothers could all have their own copy to read.

Supper ended and the children worked together to clean the dishes. Albert placed the dirty plates and spoons into a basin full of water, and Sarah scrubbed them all with a cloth. Wade wiped them dry and set them back on the shelf next to the table. Their hard work had paid off, and there was still some daylight left before they would have to go to bed. Pa sat at the table with the boys to play a game of checkers. Sarah retrieved her doll, Mandy, that she had made from a corncob. Ma sat in the rocking chair and mended a hole in Pa's shirt. With all the hard work that Pa did outside, there were almost always holes to be mended in his clothes!

Slowly the daylight faded as the sun set. Soon each of the Humphreys was sound asleep, getting the rest they needed before another day of hard work.

Review Questions:

1. What were some of the chores that the Humphrey children did?
2. What did the Humphreys do in the evening after supper?

Adventures in America Week 26

	Day 1	Day 2	Day 3
Reading	Read *The Pony Express*	Read *Buffalo Bill and Pony Bob*	Read *Smart About* pg.35 and 34
Coloring/ Activity	Coloring Page, pg. 123	"Footprint Horse" activity	Color Nevada and Nebraska on blank US map, pg. 2
Notebook	Narration from Read Aloud, history or reader, pg. 124	Copywork, pg. 125	Fill out notebook page for Nevada and Nebraska, pgs. 126, 127

Optional Read-Aloud:

Little House on the Prairie
- Day 1: Chapter 21
- Day 2: Chapter 22
- Day 3: Chapter 23
- Day 4: Chapter 24
- Day 5: Chapter 25-26

Related Picture Books:

- *They're Off! The Story of the Pony Express,* by Cheryl Harness

Possible Reader:

- *Long Way Westward*, Sandin

Activity: Footprint Horse
Materials:
-Brown, white or black construction paper
-Yarn (can be any color)
-Glue stick, scissors, markers   -Googly Eyes

•Trace student's footprints (wearing socks or shoes) onto a piece of construction paper and cut out.

•Use one to be a horse head. Glue on googly eyes. Cut out triangles of construction paper and glue on as ears.

•Glue on yarn for the horse's hair. Draw nostrils with markers.

•Glue the other footprint behind the head, to resemble a neck coming down from the head. Give your Pony Express horse a brave- sounding name!

** Optional: You may want to cut a star or blaze shape from white paper to glue onto the horse's forehead!

Optional Copywork: The mochila was the mailbag, and the riders guarded it at all costs.

Notes

The Pony Express

Before long many families were traveling west on the Oregon Trail, and new cities and villages were popping up all over the frontier. There was mail that constantly needed to go back and forth across the country. Young wives in California wrote letters describing their new babies to their dearly missed mothers back in Massachusetts. Shopkeepers wrote to businessmen telling of new wares they would like to sell. Exciting things were happening in the large, bustling cities of the East that the lonely settlers of the West wanted to hear about. These letters were anxiously awaited, but it took a very long time to carry them in a stagecoach across the vast Great Plains, through the high Rocky Mountains and over raging rivers. Often it would be nearly a month before a letter was finally delivered.

A group of smart businessmen came up with a plan to get letters and mail delivered all across the country in record time, using horseback riders instead of slow moving stagecoaches. It was a risky idea, but they thought that it just might work. For two months they bought up old buildings and built new stations, stretching out from Missouri to California. They collected 400 small horses and ponies. These horses were known to be fast and sturdy. Soon, towns for miles around hung up posters advertising a new kind of job: riding for the Pony Express!

There were station houses set up every ten miles. A rider would ride his horse or pony as fast as it could gallop over the ten miles, then just when that horse was starting to feel tired, they would arrive at the next station. The rider would quickly jump off and hop onto a different horse, which would then run as hard as it could until the following station. Each horse only had to run for ten miles before being changed for a fresh horse. But, the riders rode day and night for about one hundred miles, before stopping at a "home station." At home stations, the rider would get off his horse for the last time, handing the mail from his *mochila* to another rider who would ride the next hundred miles.

The *mochila* was the mailbag, and the riders guarded it at all costs. No matter what happened, they had promised to keep the mail safe! Along with letters and news, it also held a water bag, a Bible, a gun or two, and a horn. A rider would blow his horn loudly as he neared a station, alerting the workers there to get the next horse ready to go. Only small young men were accepted as riders for the Pony Express. If they weighed too much, the horse would get tired from his heavy load and slow down. These adventurous fellows were paid very well, but faced many dangers along the way. There was often bad weather to ride through, swift rivers, and steep mountains. Once they were hired, each rider was handed a Bible and required to promise an oath that they would not use bad language, treat animals unkindly or do anything else that was inappropriate behavior for a gentleman.

This method of mail delivery was extremely fast, but it was only used for a year and a half. After that, railroads were quickly built to span the distance, and the Pony Express faded into history. However, its story remains and adds to the adventure and excitement that was a huge part of settling the American West.

Review Questions:

1. How did the Pony Express help mail get delivered more quickly?
2. What did the Pony Express riders carry with them in their *mochilas*?

Buffalo Bill and Pony Bob

Many heroic men rode with the Pony Express, and there are several stories that have built up around these brave young riders. One fun legend says that donuts were invented because of the riders' sweethearts. These girls would carefully prepare small cakes and cookies and meet their sweetheart along the route at some point, quickly passing the treat up to him. One girl started to put holes in the middle of her little cakes so that her boyfriend could snatch them up with the barrel of his gun as he rode by her, thus creating the first donuts!

Two men stand out as especially notable figures for their daring escapades: Buffalo Bill and Pony Bob. William Cody, nicknamed "Buffalo Bill," was only fifteen years old and on his way to California when he happened to meet up with Pony Express agents along the way. Riders were required to be sixteen, but by stretching the truth, Buffalo Bill was able to sign up for the job. He is famous for managing the longest, non- stop ride ever during the Pony Express years. After having completed a long and exhausting ride, he arrived at the next station only to discover that the fellow who was supposed to continue on after him had been killed. Instead of laying down his mochila and taking a much needed night's sleep, he simply saddled up another horse and continued on for the next stretch. Riding on 21 horses for almost 24 hours straight, he accomplished more than three hundred miles of difficult trails!

Pony Bob, whose real name was Robert Haslam, has the reputation of being the most brave, re- sourceful and famous rider from the Pony Express. He was born in England and came over to America as a teenager, in time to make his mark on the settling of the Western frontier. He helped to build some of the stations for the Pony Express and then began carrying mail. One day he had an especially important piece of mail to deliver: President Lincoln's inaugural address. An inaugural address is a speech given by a new president, and just about every American likes to hear it. Since there was no television or radio to broadcast Lincoln's speech, newspapers printed it for all the people to read. While papers along the East published the speech right away, it took much longer to send it across the country to California. Pony Bob was chosen to ride part of the way for this important job.

It was an especially dangerous time. There were uprisings by a group of Native Indians along the route, and no one knew when attacks might occur. Some of the riders refused to risk traveling through such dangerous areas. This did not discourage Pony Bob. At one station, he requested to ride a horse called "Old Buck." Old Buck may not have been the fastest horse around, but he had seen battles with Native Indians before and knew how to fight. For awhile, there was no one to be seen and Pony Bob breathed a sigh of relief that his job would be easier than he had expected. Eventually, however, ambushes were all around him. Laying flat on Old Buck, Pony Bob rode on with arrows and bullets whizzing by him. He managed to defend himself against most of the attackers, but one arrow hit his arm. Riding on, another arrow pierced his jaw, knocking out several of his teeth.

Pony Bob is known for his bravery for a reason- he rode on and on! After arriving at the next sta- tion, he allowed his wounds to be quickly cleaned before swinging back onto his saddle and riding out to finish his route. Against all odds, the inaugural address of President Lincoln was safely delivered to Califor- nia in record time. Normally the Pony Express could bring mail to the coast in ten days, but this important letter arrived in less than eight!

Review Questions:

1. What were the names of two famous Pony Express riders?
2. What did Pony Bob do after he had been hit by arrows during the attack?

Adventures in America Week 27

	Day 1	Day 2	Day 3
Reading	Read *The Gold Rush*	Read *Gold Fever*	Read *Smart About* pg.13
Coloring/ Activity	Coloring Page, pg. 129	"Pan for Gold" activity	Color Colorado on blank US map, pg. 2
Notebook	Narration from Read Aloud, history or reader, pg. 130	Copywork, pg. 131	Fill out notebook page for Colorado, pg. 132

Optional Read-Aloud:

On the Banks of Plum Creek
- Day 1: Chapter 1
- Day 2: Chapter 2
- Day 3: Chapter 3-4
- Day 4: Chapter 5
- Day 5: Chapter 6

Related Picture Books:

- *Gold Fever!*, by Rosalyn Schanzer

Possible Reader:

- *Buffalo Bill and the Pony Express*, Coerr

Activity: Pan for Gold
Materials:
-About two handfuls of stones and rocks
-Shallow pan such as a metal pie plate (or if you have a sieve, even better!)
Metallic gold paint   -Sink, tub or large container

•Help your student paint several of the stones metallic gold.

•Once dry, mix up the painted stones with the rest of the unpainted stones in a sink, tub or large container. Fill up partially with water.

•Let your student use the pan to "pan" for gold. Dip it into some of the stones and shake them around to see what was found. Maybe they'll strike it rich!

Optional Copywork: California was given the nickname "The Golden State."

Notes

The Gold Rush

James Marshall thought it was just another ordinary day in January working with his friend at Sutter's Mill. He had come to California several years ago on a wagon train, hoping to make his fortune. After working for Mr. Sutter by making tools, furniture, spinning wheels and other things from wood, the two men had decided to open up a sawmill together. Using a mill that was powered by water from the American River, they cut rough logs into boards that were used for building houses, wagons and other things. James Marshall suspected that the mill was not working properly, and he was closely examining the river bed underneath it. He looked, but he did not see anything that would cause a problem. He did see something, though! As he peered into the water, some shining flecks caught his eye. Squinting to take a better look, Marshall could see that there were indeed some bright, golden rocks amongst the stones covering the bed of the river. He bent over and scooped up a handful to inspect more closely. Could it possibly be what he suspected? He pressed it with a rock and found that it was somewhat soft. All of a sudden, he caught his breath. It had to be! In the American River at Sutter's Mill, James Marshall had discovered gold!

Marshall performed some more simple tests so he could know for sure that the mineral was indeed gold, and not just "fool's gold." Fool's Gold was a rock that looked just like gold and had tricked many people. All of the experiments proved that he had the genuine thing. Finally he showed it to Sutter, expecting to see his partner jump up and down in excitement. Instead, Sutter simply shook his head in dismay.

"They'll all come here! To my land, our mill. We will be ruined!" Sutter stated quietly.

The two partners agreed to keep it a secret for awhile. Months passed and still nobody knew that gold had been found at Sutter's Mill. Finally, rumors got out and one day the truth was printed in the newspaper. Still, no one paid much attention until the day when a storekeeper came running into the streets yelling that gold had been found in the American River! The clever businessman had first stocked his store full of gold-prospecting supplies such as picks and pans that could be used to find gold at the bottom of water. Once he was all ready for the customers to come and buy them, he announced to the people that the gold was there, waiting to be found.

All at once the small town of San Francisco was completely emptied as its people poured out carrying their newly purchased prospecting supplies and running to the American River. Shopkeepers locked up their stores, farmers dropped their shovels and left their livestock; even women left their pastry dough sitting on the table to rush into the action. Poor Sutter looked on sadly as every one of his workers deserted him, eager to try their luck and make a fortune. It was just the beginning, like a tiny match that would set light to an enormous bonfire. California, and the United States, would be forever changed by Marshall's discovery!

Review Questions:

1. Where did James Marshall find gold?
2. What did people do when they heard about his discovery?

Gold Fever

San Francisco stood nearly empty for awhile as its townspeople zealously staked areas of the American River for themselves. They dipped their pans down again and again, looking for the precious metal. Searching for gold this way was called "panning for gold." The hunt for gold also had another name: "prospecting." At first, the prospectors were very lucky and found large pieces of gold sitting right on top of the riverbed in plain sight. Every day it seemed like someone was striking it rich and making more money than they had ever seen. This spurred on the others, who anxiously worked and waited for their turn to make their fortune.

By August, the news had come out in newspapers back east. At first the people were not sure what to believe. After all, it sounded too good to be true. However, the news kept coming that more and more people were getting rich. It must be that there really was gold to be found in the American River! By 1849, thousands of men, women and families were leaving the comforts and safety of East Coast city life for the hardships and adventures that lay along the Oregon Trail all the way to California. So many came that the group was called by their own special nickname: the forty-niners, because it was the year 1849.

It was diagnosed that almost the whole world was infected with gold fever! They did not just come on the Oregon Trail from the Eastern United States. They sailed in ships up from Mexico and South America. They sailed all the way from Europe and even from Asia! People who did not speak a word of English arrived with their entire families, abandoning the ships in the harbor and rushing as fast as they possibly could to the American River. They all wanted a chance to find gold before it had all been discovered by someone else.

Not everyone found gold. Most people never made much money. But there were fortunes made, and not just by the prospectors. Clever businessmen made lots of money by selling food and supplies to the prospectors, and by testing and weighing the gold. California was given the nickname of "The Golden State." People everywhere were talking about the California Dream, which was that anyone could get rich if they worked hard and were lucky. Because of the rush to get out west, railroads were speedily built and steamboats were quickly put into action. More and more people were willing to settle in the Western states and territories. Not only did San Francisco grow from a little town to a huge, booming city, but with so many people coming from other countries to the United States, the whole country grew as a result!

James Marshall could not possibly have imagined how that little gold nugget he had first found would change the face of the nation forever!

Review Questions:

1. What were people called who searched for gold?
2. What became California's nickname?

Adventures in America Week 28

	Day 1	Day 2	Day 3
Reading	Read *Slavery in a Free Nation*	Read *Here Comes the Cotton Gin*	Read *Smart About* pg.41 and 48
Coloring/ Activity	Coloring Page, pg. 133	"Johnnycakes" activity	Color North Dakota and South Dakota on blank US map, pg. 2
Notebook	Narration from Read Aloud, history or reader, pg. 134	Copywork, pg. 135	Fill out notebook page for North Dakota and South Dakota, pgs. 136, 137

Optional Read-Aloud:

On the Banks of Plum Creek
- Day 1: Chapter 7
- Day 2: Chapter 8
- Day 3: Chapter 9-10
- Day 4: Chapter 11
- Day 5: Chapter 12

Related Picture Books:

- *Who Owns the Sun?*, by Stacy Chbosky

Possible Reader:

- *Buffalo Bill and the Pony Express*, Coerr

Activity: Johnnycakes

Materials:
- 2 Cups stone ground cornmeal
- 4 T. butter
- 2 T. boiling water
- 1tsp. salt
- 1 Cup whole milk

- Heat a greased skillet on the stove, or use an electric griddle.

- Cream cornmeal, salt and butter together.

- Add milk and enough water to make a firm batter.

- Drop large spoonfuls onto the hot skillet or griddle. Flatten slightly with the back of a spoon.

- Turn and cook on other side.

- Serve with lots of butter and enjoy!

Optional Copywork: For many slaves, life was filled with fear and heartache.

Notes

Slavery in a Free Nation

Although freedom is something that Americans have always loved, there was a time when many of her people were not free at all. Since the first settlers had arrived in Virginia, ships full of slaves had been delivered there as well. These were almost always men and women who had been taken from their homes in Africa or other places, and then were sold as slaves to do different kinds of hard work for their masters.

As the colonies grew and then became states, most slaves were moved down to the South. The South was just right for growing expensive crops like tobacco, cotton and sugar cane. The summers are long and hot, and the winters rarely get very cold. The soil is rich and fertile, perfect for farming. Huge plantations sprung up all over the South. Plantations were large farms. Besides the beautiful white columned plantation house where the owner's family lived, there were many other buildings which held farm equipment and housed slaves.

For many slaves, life was filled with fear and heartache. They were forced to do hard work from sun-up to sun-down, often without enough food to eat. If they did not work hard enough or fast enough, they could be harshly punished. Disobeying an order, talking back to a master or trying to run away could mean heavy discipline. They often lived with the fear that their families might be torn apart if one of them was sold to another owner. With new frontiers being settled, large groups of slaves were moved in chains across the weary miles. Many times, a husband would be forced to go without his wife, or children would be left behind with grandparents. Owners had complete control over their slaves, and could make them do anything they wanted.

In the South, many people never questioned whether slavery was right or wrong. Many thought slavery was an acceptable part of life, and knew that their huge plantations could never grow so many crops without the slaves working in the fields. However, there were lots of Americans in the North and South who were against slavery and knew that it was wrong. Many argued that if "all men are created equal," then slaves should be considered equal, too. As time went by, more and more people began to speak out against slavery. These people were called "abolitionists." All kinds of people became abolitionists, and many of them did heroic things to help set slaves free.

Review Questions:

1. What is a plantation?
2. Why were slaves' lives difficult?

Here Comes the Cotton Gin

As time went by, fewer people kept slaves. Many fair minded people set their slaves free, as George Washington had done. In the North, it was often too expensive to buy and feed slaves, and so hiring servants and workers made more sense. In the South, the expensive crops like tobacco and cotton were getting harder to grow. Tobacco didn't make as much money as it used to, and cotton was so difficult to harvest. Once it came in, workers had to pick out all the seeds before the owners could sell it. Cotton plantations were pretty small and only kept a few slaves.

That was until a man named Eli Whitney arrived in Georgia. One day he was walking outside and noticed a hungry cat trying to make off with a nice, plump chicken. The chicken was inside a fence, and the cat eagerly eyed it from the other side. Finally, the cat was able to grab the chicken. Try as he might, he just could not get that chicken through the fence. A few feathers were all his hungry mouth could manage. The chicken eventually made it to the shelter of his coop to calm his nerves, with only some feathers missing.

As Eli Whitney watched this scene unfold, a new idea struck him! If only they could get the seeds out of picked cotton more easily, then the plantations could grow plenty of cotton and make more money. He set out to invent a special device that he named a "cotton gin." The "gin" was short for engine. Basically, it was a wooden drum that pulled cotton fibers through, but was not big enough for the seeds. Just like the cat was only able to get some fluff and feathers from the chicken, the cotton gin would only take the nice cotton and leave the seeds behind. This worked much faster than having workers go through all the cotton and pick out the seeds by hand.

At the same time, big factories were being built in the Northern states and across the ocean in Europe. These factories had new machines and were able to take cotton and turn it into fabric more quickly than ever. They just needed more cotton, and they needed it fast! All of a sudden, the South needed to grow heaps and heaps more cotton to sell to the North and Europe. How could they grow enough? They needed more slaves.

Sadly, because of the new cotton gin, more and more slaves were needed to do the hard work of clearing land for fields, plowing dirt, sowing seeds and picking cotton. The owners of big plantations bought as many strong, sturdy men as they could afford. Soon the South was making more money than ever before with their expensive crop "King Cotton." Unfortunately, all the work was being accomplished by the slaves. Abolitionists, the people who believed slavery was wrong, were appalled. They would find a way to help those men and women become free, even if it meant doing it "underground."

Review Questions:

1. What was Eli Whitney's invention?
2. What were the people who did not agree with slavery called?

Adventures in America Week 29

	Day 1	Day 2	Day 3
Reading	Read *The Underground Railroad*	Read *Two Slaves Make a Difference*	Read *Smart About* pg.33
Coloring/ Activity	Coloring Page, pg. 139	"Quilt Code" activity	Color Montana on blank US map, pg. 2
Notebook	Narration from Read Aloud, history or reader, pg. 140	Copywork, pg. 141	Fill out notebook page for Montana, pg. 142

Optional Read-Aloud:

On the Banks of Plum Creek
- Day 1: Chapter 13
- Day 2: Chapter 14-15
- Day 3: Chapter 16
- Day 4: Chapter 17
- Day 5: Chapter 18-19

Related Picture Books:

- *Follow the Drinking Gourd,* by Jeanette Winter

Possible Reader:

- *The Drinking Gourd*, Monjo

Optional Copywork: The Underground Railroad was an invisible train that connected safe houses by secret routes.

Activity: Quilt Code
You can choose whether to invent your own quilt pattern or choose one of the actual Underground Railroad patterns from this website: http://www.osblackhistory.com/quiltcodes.php

Materials:
-Construction paper (several colors)
-Glue sticks
-Scissors, pencil

•Plan the design you will make OR have your student choose from the designs from the website, discussing the names and what each symbolized.

•Select the colors you will use, and draw the shapes in pencil on your paper.

•Cut out the shapes, and let your student arrange them on a solid background before gluing them onto the paper.

•You can also make holes at each end and attach ribbon to hang your quilt from a doorknob.

Notes

The Underground Railroad

With the arrival of the cotton gin, more slaves than ever were working on the cotton plantations of the South. Abolitionists, people who believed slavery was wrong, knew something had to be done. They worked together with freed blacks to create a way for slaves in the South to escape up into Northern states or Canada, where they could be free.

The Underground Railroad was not really a train track at all! In fact, most people had no idea where it was, because they could not actually see it with their eyes. It was an invisible train that connected safe houses by secret routes. If a slave dared to escape from his master, he could travel at night along the routes which led through forests and by streams. Certain houses held people who were willing to help the runaways. These people hid the slaves in their barns, cellars or back rooms. The slaves would receive food for their hungry stomachs and a place to rest. As soon as darkness fell, they continued on their journey. It was dangerous because there were slave catchers nearby. They prowled the states all the way up to the Canadian border, relentlessly pursuing runaways. There was plenty of money to be made by returning these slaves to their masters.

Of course, nobody could talk openly about the Underground Railroad, or else the safe houses would be discovered and the runaways would be caught. In order to describe the routes, different forms of secret codes were used. Sometimes songs were sung by workers in the fields of the plantations. These songs may sound innocent, but the words were actually secret codes telling which way to travel on the Underground Railroad. Some songs described following the "Drinking Gourd," which was another name for the Big Dipper constellation in the night sky. Using the stars as a map, runaways could navigate their way North. Signals, such as hooting like an owl, were used to make sure a safe house was truly safe.

One legend tells of quilts being used as codes. Seamstresses sewed quilts using different patterns. The patterns looked like they were just pretty shapes, but they actually had meanings. The Wrench pattern meant they should gather up their tools and prepare to leave. The Bear's Paw told slaves to head North over the Appalachian Mountains and follow actual bear tracks, which would lead them to water and food. Flying Geese were a signal to follow the direction of geese migrating North in the spring. The Sailboat implied water was nearby and there would be boats available for crossing. A Bow Tie meant the runaways should change clothes into a disguise, and the Log Cabin assured them there was a safe house nearby. These quilts were hung on porches as if they were just drying in the sun, and nobody suspected their hidden meanings. Most slaves could not read or write, so using patterns and pictures was a way of guiding them to freedom.

Review Questions:

1. Was the Underground Railroad a train track?
2. How were quilts used to help runaway slaves?

Two Slaves Make a Difference

Harriet Tubman was born as a slave in Maryland. She first heard about the Underground Railroad when she was eleven years old. The stories of men and women who had dared to leave the homes of their masters intrigued her. Once she had grown up, she decided she had been a slave long enough. By following the Underground Railroad she was able to travel north to freedom. Running away was difficult, but after doing it successfully once, she knew she wanted to help others escape, too. She quietly snuck back onto the plantations where her parents and sister lived, helping them find the courage to run away. Before long, she was traveling back and forth, north and south, helping other slaves to escape. They called her "Grandma Moses." Just like the Moses in the Bible who helped lead the Israelites out of Egypt, Grandma Moses was guiding her people out of slavery! Although slave catchers searched and searched for her, nobody knew where she was or how she traveled. Just about every single slave who went with her completed the journey safely and became free.

Another very important man, named Frederick Douglas, was also born as a slave. His mother worked long hours in a cornfield, so he was sent to live with his grandmother in a little cabin near the plantation. He was happy there and enjoyed playing freely in the woods. One day, Grandma told him it was time to take a journey. He walked along fearfully, clinging to her skirts. Eventually they reached a plantation with a large, beautiful house. Frederick would be living in a little hut near the house, and would learn to do the hard work of a slave. Many people liked Frederick because he was friendly and had a nice smile. Before long, his masters sent him to live in the city where he would only have to help with housework and looking after a small baby. This sounded pleasant to Frederick. It would be easier than farm work.

In the city, Frederick played with the little baby and ran errands for the mother. The mother was a kind woman who decided to teach Frederick to read and write. He was eager to learn and could quickly read simple words. His mistress beamed in pride and excitely told her husband about their smart slave. She expected to see her husband's face light up with joy, but instead clouds formed on his brow. He informed her sternly that slaves were not allowed to learn reading and writing, because if they became educated they might decide not to obey their masters anymore. His wife obeyed his wishes, and Frederick's lessons stopped. His desire to learn continued to grow, though, and so he began asking little children in the neighborhood to teach him. He offered pieces of bread as payment. Whenever he had the chance, he read newspapers or any books he could find. He thought to himself that if knowledge was the way to freedom, he wanted to learn as much as he could!

Little Frederick grew up. One day, he changed into a disguise to look like a sailor and he ran away. Once he was safe, he used all his time to help other slaves become free. His house was part of the Underground Railroad, and runaways knew he would help them. He traveled around, telling people about his life as a slave. Many people in the North had never spoken to a slave before and did not know how badly some slaves were treated. Frederick Douglas showed people the truth about slavery, and helped people decide that it was indeed wrong.

Review Questions:

1. What was Harriet Tubman's nickname?
2. Why were slaves not allowed to learn to read and write?

Adventures in America Week 30

	Day 1	Day 2	Day 3
Reading	Read *Abraham Lincoln*	Read *President Abraham Lincoln*	Read *Smart About* pg.54 and 19
Coloring/ Activity	Coloring Page, pg. 143	"Abraham Lincoln Hat" activity	Color Washington and Idaho on blank US map, pg. 2
Notebook	Narration from Read Aloud, history or reader, pg. 144	Copywork, pg. 145	Fill out notebook page for Washington and Idaho, pgs. 146, 147

Optional Read-Aloud:

On the Banks of Plum Creek
- Day 1: Chapter 20
- Day 2: Chapter 21
- Day 3: Chapter 22-23
- Day 4: Chapter 24
- Day 5: Chapter 25-26

Related Picture Books:

- *Abraham Lincoln*, by Ingri & Edgar Parin D'Aulaire

Possible Reader:

- *The Drinking Gourd*, Monjo

Optional Copywork: Abraham Lincoln soon earned the nickname "Honest Abe."

Activity: Abraham Lincoln Hat

Materials:
-Paper plate   -Black paint
-1 Piece of black felt   -Scissors
-2 Pieces of black construction paper
-Glue (hot glue gun or craft glue is best)

•Cut the center out of the paper plate and paint the rim black.

•Staple 2 pieces of black construction paper together (on the shorter ends).

•Cut two 2 inch wide strips from the felt.

•Once plate is dry, roll the construction paper so that it fits onto the paper plate circle. Trim to correct size and staple together. Remove from plate.

•**Carefully** spread hot glue or craft glue around the bottom edge of the construction paper and gently fit onto plate rim. Gently press together, holding for about thirty seconds in order for glue to hold.

•Place hot glue or craft glue on the two strips of felt. Gently press the pieces around the hat, just above the rim.

•Wait until completely dry and then let your student have fun being Abraham Lincoln!

Notes

Abraham Lincoln

Young Abraham Lincoln, or Abe as his father called him, was born in a little one room cabin in the woods of Kentucky. Like all of the neighbors around him, the Lincolns' home had a dirt floor. Before Abe was two years old, the family moved to Knob Creek Farm. Their new cabin was just as tiny, but the land surrounding it was absolutely beautiful! A crystal clear creek flowed through the property. There were steep grassy hills called "knobs" on both sides of the land. Abraham and his older sister, Sarah, could play in the grass and creek when they were not busy planting corn and pumpkins with their father. Abraham loving playing, hunting and fishing, just like any other little boy in Kentucky.

When Abe was seven years old, his father decided they should move out of Kentucky to the state of Indiana. His father did not like slavery and wanted to live in a free state. In Indiana, they moved to a place that was still all wilderness. The thick forests were full of bears and panthers. The Lincolns worked together hunting for food. Abraham once shot a wild turkey, but then felt badly afterwards and decided that hunting was not for him. Through hard work, the family cleared the land into fields for farming.

Soon after moving, Abraham's mother caught a terrible disease that was called milk sickness. Something the cows ate made their milk dangerous, and many people became sick. After being in bed for a week, their mother finally died. The children were heartbroken. Before long, their father remarried a kind and loving woman. This stepmother became a close friend to Abraham and took wonderful care of her new children, along with the children she already had.

With a new stepmother to organize the home and nurture the children, Abraham had a joyous and happy boyhood. One day, his parents decided that he should have some schooling. Not everyone went to school in those days, and most people could not write. At school, Abraham learned some spelling, a little writing and how to read simple words. He proved to be a very hard worker with an appetite for learning. After a few months, he stopped attending the school. At home he continued to read through his spelling book on his own and carefully copied out sentences until he had learned them perfectly. He did go to school one more time, but all of his time spent there only added up to less than one year. Everything else that he learned was through studying and teaching himself at home.

Abraham loved to read! He spent all of his free time lying on the floor with his long legs propped up and a book in his hand. Some of his favorite books were Aesop's Fables and Pilgrim's Progress. He read certain parts of books over and over again until he had memorized them. He would copy down sentences that he especially liked, writing on wooden boards if there was no paper nearby. With his stepmother's encouragement, his own perseverance and hard work, and a quick mind, Abraham Lincoln was able to read and learn more on his own than many others ever learn from years of schooling.

Review Questions:

1. What kind of a house did Abraham Lincoln live in when he was a child?
2. What kind of schooling did Abraham Lincoln have?

President Abraham Lincoln

The young Abraham Lincoln grew up, and up, and up! He kept on growing until he was taller than most men. In fact, below his pants there was always about six inches of bare shins showing through! It was indeed a difficult task for his stepmother to make pants long enough to fit him.

Once he had grown, he moved away from home and went to work on a river barge. He liked that job because he was able to take the boat up and down the river delivering goods, and he met all kinds of interesting people on the way. Although he did not see many slaves where he lived, he always remembered the time his own barge floated by a boat full of slaves who had been sold to a different owner. The men were all chained together for their journey.

After working along the river for awhile, Abraham Lincoln moved to a different town and tried working as a shopkeeper. He enjoyed this job, too, because it gave him plenty of time to do his favorite things: read the newspapers and talk to neighbors. He never lost his appetite for reading and was especially interested in politics and how the state of Illinois was growing. The neighbors all loved talking to the tall Abe Lincoln. Whatever they talked about, he would always have a funny story or joke to add to the conversation. However, Abraham did not like business and found it hard to make any money working in a store. Eventually, he left that job behind, too.

Soon he found the perfect job for someone who loved reading, had a quick mind, and was good at talking to people. He became a lawyer! A lawyer is someone who studies the laws of the state and country, and then finds ways to help solve people's problems. To be a good lawyer requires lots of time studying and reading, just what Abraham Lincoln loved to do! He also had to stand up in court and argue that the person he was helping was right. Since he was so good at talking and arguing, he won almost all of his cases. Some lawyers found it hard to win a case and still be honest. But Abraham Lincoln was committed to the truth and soon earned the nickname "Honest Abe." Abraham Lincoln married a girl named Mary, who was from Kentucky just like him! They had four children, and he was a very loving father. He often brought his sons to the office with him, letting them play with the inkstand and papers. For many, many years Abraham Lincoln practiced law and became well known. He was also involved in politics and had many good ideas about ways to make America better.

One day, the people of America had a vote and decided that Honest Abe should be the president of the United States! This was an extremely important job for the Lincolns. It was also extremely difficult because it was one of the hardest times in America's history. The Southern states and the Northern states were arguing. Northern states wanted to end slavery and were angry with the large Southern cotton plantations. The South decided they wanted to leave the Union. There would be a war. It would be a great challenge to see if President Abraham Lincoln would be able to keep the country from dividing.

Review Questions:

1. What kinds of jobs did Abraham Lincoln have?
2. What was Abraham Lincoln's nickname?

Adventures in America Week 31

	Day 1	**Day 2**	**Day 3**
Reading	Read *North and South*	Read *Gettysburg Address*	Read *Smart About* pg.57
Coloring/ Activity	Coloring Page, pg. 149	"Soap on a Rope" activity	Color Wyoming on blank US map, pg. 2
Notebook	Narration from Read Aloud, history or reader, pg. 150	Copywork, pg. 151	Fill out notebook page for Wyoming, pg. 152

Optional Read-Aloud:

On the Banks of Plum Creek
- Day 1: Chapter 27-28
- Day 2: Chapter 29-30
- Day 3: Chapter 31
- Day 4: Chapter 32
- Day 5: Chapter 33-34

Related Picture Books:

- *Just a Few Words, Mr. Lincoln*, by Jean Fritz

Possible Reader:

- *Dust for Dinner*, Turner

Optional Copywork: The Civil War was fought between the North and the South.

Activity: Soap on a Rope

Making soap was actually a much more involved process than you will have to do for this activity! Soap flakes make it a convenient at- home project.

Materials:
-3 Cups soap flakes (can use Ivory Snow detergent, or make your own flakes by grating bars of pure soap)
-Food coloring   -Vegetable oil
-Bowl and water   -Piece of string (about 12 in.)

•Pour soap flakes into a large bowl.

•Add a few drops food coloring to 1 cup of water. Pour over soap flakes.

•Let your student use their hands to mix the soap until it has the consistency of play dough. Add more water if needed.

•Tie the ends of your string together.

•Rub a drop of vegetable oil into the palms of your student's hands and let him shape the soap around the knotted end, so that a loop of string is hanging out of the soap.

•Let stand overnight to set.

•Carry your soap on a rope to your next bath time!

Notes

North and South

William loved living in Boston and thought it must be the best city in all of the North. From what he had heard, the North was full of big, bustling cities just like Boston. William could understand why so many people liked living in these crowded places. There was always something exciting to see or hear about or do! Why, just on the one main street downtown there were stores, houses, schools, hospitals, factories, banks and churches. The noise on the streets from the people and horses was almost deafening. Every day, William left school at lunch time and savored the air of excitement as he walked home for his meal. These days, there were always groups of men huddled together, talking anxiously about the rising tensions between the North and the South.

William grinned smugly. Probably, there would never be a war. After all, now they had President Abraham Lincoln to show them who was in charge! President Lincoln would certainly put an end to slavery. Why, what would they ever want to secede for? William felt proud to have learned that new word from his father last night. Now he understood that the Southern states wanted to actually leave the Union. William shook his head just considering it. Soon he had arrived home where his mother was ready with some delicious beef stew and crusty bread, William's favorite meal!

At that same time, miles and miles away in the South, Susannah was also about to enjoy her midday meal. She walked up the lane leading to the wide front porch, or verandah, that wrapped all the way around her family's large plantation home. Walking the red clay paths and gazing out at the lush rows of cotton was one of her favorite pastimes. She loved to breathe in the sweet smell of honeysuckle. It was nice to be outside where you might feel a gentle breeze come ease away the heat. Even though summer had not quite arrived, the air was already muggy and hot. As she passed through the door, a house slave ushered her to the dining room table.

Having slaves in and outside the house was a normal part of life for Susannah, something she had grown up knowing. She loved Molly, the slave who had lovingly taken care of Susannah ever since she was a baby. In fact, Susannah could not imagine why anyone would think slavery was wrong. Lately the men in the county had been talking loudly about the Northerners who wanted to put an end to slavery. This made their blood boil! Without slaves working in the fields, how in the world could they grow enough cotton? Factories up North and in Europe wanted more and more cotton all the time. Didn't they understand that slavery was an important part of all of their lives? Susannah had heard the men and young boys boasting about how grand it would be to secede- leave the Union. Susannah always listened with pride, sure that with such strong, brave men leading the way, the South was sure to win any war! Susannah took her seat at the dining room table and surveyed the spread of hot fried chicken, biscuits and collard greens. Her stomach growled and she smiled in anticipation.

Review Questions:

1. How did people in the North feel about slavery?
2. What did Susannah think would happen if there was a war?

Gettysburg Address

It was certainly a difficult time for a president. President Abraham Lincoln had the challenging task of keeping America from dividing. Soon the country was at war. President Lincoln issued the Emancipation Proclamation, stating that slaves were to be set free. Some slaves immediately left their masters, crying tears of joy that they had lived to see such a happy day! Many slaves went to fight on the side of the North in the war. Others chose to stay and continue working where they were. This "war between the states" was a civil war, which is a war that is between two sides of the same country. Frederick Douglas, the former slave who had helped so many slaves escape, urged men to join and fight. In return for doing the hard work of a soldier, these men were offered freedom and payment.

The Civil War lasted four years and there were battles in many states. Everyone held their breath in suspense over which side would finally win. First, it seemed that the South was winning, and then the North. Next, it would appear that the South would take victory, only to have the North win the next battle. It was a terrible war, with lots and lots of men losing their lives on the battlefield. The men went to war, and the women helped all they could. Women became nurses and took care of wounded soldiers. They sewed bandages, uniforms, flags and whatever else was needed. Both in the North and the South, the women stood behind their men bravely, supporting them with all their hearts.

The North won a very important battle at Gettysburg. The Battle of Gettysburg would end up helping the North win the war. But even though they had won, many men had been killed. It was decided that they should have a special soldier's cemetery nearby to honor the graves of these courageous war heroes. The cemetery was built, and President Abraham Lincoln was invited to come say a few words to remember the men who had died. He arrived in Gettysburg the night before the ceremony and stayed at his friend's house on the town square. Early the next morning, he rode upon his chestnut horse and joined the throng of people headed toward the cemetery. An enormous group of politicians, widows and townspeople eagerly joined the ceremony.

There was music, prayers and speeches. Finally President Lincoln stepped up onto the platform. He gazed out at the crowds of people. They were saddened by the loss of these soldiers, yet proud of the battle they had fought. President Lincoln lifted his voice and gave his speech. It is remembered as the Gettysburg Address, and is one of the most well known American speeches ever given! This is what he said: (See Page 143)

Review Questions:

1. What was the war between the states called?
2. What was the name of the famous speech that President Lincoln gave?

Adventures in America Week 32

	Day 1	Day 2	Day 3
Reading	Read *Railroads West*	Read *The Last Spike*	Read *Smart About* pg.51 and 43
Coloring/ Activity	Coloring Page, pg. 153	"Gold Spike" activity	Color Utah and Oklahoma on blank US map, pg. 2
Notebook	Narration from Read Aloud, history or reader, pg. 154	Copywork, pg. 155	Fill out notebook page for Utah and Oklahoma, pgs. 156, 157

Optional Read-Aloud:

On the Banks of Plum Creek
- Day 1: Chapter 35-36
- Day 2: Chapter 37
- Day 3: Chapter 38
- Day 4: Chapter 39-40
- Day 5: Chapter 41

Related Picture Books:

- *Ten Mile Day and the Building of the Transcontinental Railroad,* by Mary Ann Fraser

Possible Reader:

- *Dust for Dinner*, Turner

Activity: Gold Spike

Materials:
- Stiff cardboard
- Metallic gold paint
- Nail, toothpick or other sharp object
- Pencil, scissors

• Draw a spike shape on the cardboard. Make it 8 in. long and about 2 in. wide, with a wide rounded disk on top (like the head of a nail) and tapering down to a point at the other end. Cut out the spike.

• Let your student paint the spike metallic gold.

• Once dry, let them use a nail or toothpick to etch their name or a design on the flattened sides of the spike.

Optional Copywork: With a new railroad to connect the two sides of America, more and more people would be moving to the West.

Notes

Railroads West

Chen gazed back at the miles and miles of railroad track that had been laid. He had come to America five years ago. Leaving his small fishing village in China had been sad, but exciting, too! The men who had come to his village worked for the Union Pacific Railroad company. They were searching for new recruits, men who would leave their families, brave the voyage over the ocean, and do the hard work of laying down rails for the train track. These men were offered one dollar a day, for working from sunup to sundown. Plenty of men from China had eagerly jumped at the opportunity to make money in a foreign land.

At first, the difficult work of laying track had almost been too much for Chen. He had spent his whole life on the coast of Southern China, where the air was warm and balmy. Here, the winters were bleak with a cold that chilled his bones and stiffened his fingers. Snowstorms blew up suddenly, with the freezing wind snapping in their faces and whipping against the tents. Summer was not much better. The blazing sun burned their skin and left the men feeling fatigued and exhausted before the day was even half through. By now, Chen had grown accustomed to the severe weather and the rough terrain of the land. He found the Rocky Mountains breathtakingly beautiful, and admired the huge blue expanse of sky that stretched over the prairies. America was certainly a beautiful country.

Chen had been hired along with many more Chinese, Irish and American workers to accomplish a huge dream. So far, crossing from the East to the West coast of the country was a very difficult task, taking six months or more on a covered wagon. The two sides of the country felt so far apart that there may as well have been an ocean between them. The railroad companies had devised a plan that would connect the two coasts by a single railroad track. There were already plenty of railroads winding their way between the cities and towns in the East. What was needed was a track that started at one of the train stations in the East and went all the way through the wilderness, over the prairies, the deserts, and the Rocky Mountains to California. They called it the Transcontinental Railroad. It would be a humongous job, but with enough workers, it could be done. But finding workers was more challenging than they expected. There just were not enough men in the West to do the job. Finally, the railroad companies decided to hire more men from China. Chinese workers had proven to be extremely hard working and smart. Boats were sent to China to bring back more workers. Chen had arrived on one of those boats.

It was not just an opportunity to make money. It was also the chance to be part of building up a country. With a new railroad to connect the two sides of America, more and more people would be moving to the West. New towns would be built, new businesses would be needed. It would be the perfect time to start a new life in the new land. Chen was thrilled to be included in the growth of this exciting nation!

Review Questions:

1. Where was Chen from?
2. What was the Transcontinental Railroad?

The Last Spike

The month was May. The place was Promontory, Utah. Chen felt nervous with anticipation. After six years of grueling labor in the midst of incredible dangers and hardships, the entire track had been laid. One line stretched from California. The other line came from the East. They met together at Promontory Summit, in Utah. Working in a kind of feverish excitement, the men on both sides had gone faster and faster, anxious to reach the meeting point. Today would be the day! The entire track had been laid, and now all that remained was to drive one last spike. It called for a ceremony of celebration!

There was certainly much cause for celebrating. Chen thought soberly of the men who had been injured or killed over the years. Besides the harsh extremes of the weather, there had been numerous accidents from black powder. The black powder was an explosive that had been used to blow up granite rock when carving tunnels through the massive mountains. Others had hurt themselves using the giant, heavy sledgehammers to drive the spikes.

However, there had been many good days as well! There had been days that were like this sunny, breezy day in May. Days when the sky was incredibly blue and the landscape took your breath away. Most of the time, the men were all alone in the vast wilderness. Once in awhile, they came upon a small town. Many of these towns were "towns on wheels." They were brought along the tracks, moving along with the railroad workers. In these little, makeshift towns there were restaurants, games and shops. A few remained where they had begun, becoming permanent towns that still exist today. Most disappeared without a trace once the tracks had been laid.

On this day in May, hundreds of railroad workers, government officials and townspeople gathered at Promontory Summit. A group of eight Chinese men laid the last rail, to the applause of the crowds. A golden spike was brought forth, engraved on every side. One of the quotes read "May God continue the unity of our Country, as this Railroad unites the two great Oceans of the world." As the golden spike was driven into the rail, a single word, "DONE," was telegraphed throughout the country. Yesterday it had taken six months in a covered wagon to cross the continent; tomorrow it would take six days on a steam powered train.

Today, Chen thought, was the end and the beginning. The hard work was finished. A new railroad line had been born. Hundreds of Chinese had moved to America and would choose to stay. More and more people would travel on the train from the crowded East to the growing West. America would never be the same!

Review Questions:

1. What were some of the challenges the workers faced while building the railroads?
2. What material was used to make the last spike?

Adventures in America Week 33

	Day 1	Day 2	Day 3
Reading	Read *John Henry*	Read *Stormalong*	Read *Smart About* pg.38
Coloring/ Activity	Coloring Page, pg. 159	"Painted Hammer" activity	Color New Mexico on blank US map, pg. 2
Notebook	Narration from Read Aloud, history or reader, pg. 160	Copywork, pg. 161	Fill out notebook page for New Mexico, pg. 162

Optional Read-Aloud:

In Grandma's Attic
- Day 1: Intro, Chapter 1
- Day 2: Chapter 2
- Day 3: Chapter 3
- Day 4: Chapter 4-5
- Day 5: Chapter 6

Related Picture Books:

- *John Henry,* by Ezra Jack Keats

Possible Reader:

- *Prairie School,* Avi

Activity: Painted Hammer

Let your student decorate their own special hammer! Even if they weren't "born with a hammer in their hand," they will enjoy this activity.

Materials:
-Small, lightweight hammer with a wooden handle (inexpensively available at dollar stores and other places)
-Acrylic paints   -Paintbrush

•Lay down newspaper to protect the surface of your table.

•Place various colors of paint in front of your child. Let them decorate the handle of their hammer however they wish. Let dry.

•With careful adult supervision, let your student practice using their hammer with some nails and a small piece of wood.

Optional Copywork: John Henry was born with a hammer in his hand.

NOTE For the next two weeks you will be reading about American tall tales. I chose to include these because they serve as a significant part of America's history and cultural heritage. Johnny Appleseed and Davy Crockett were actual historical men. The others probably have little or no basis in fact, but are enjoyable stories about well-known figures. Please make sure to explain to your student the difference between legend and fact.

Notes

John Henry

John Henry was born during the years before the Civil War. His family worked as slaves on a large cotton plantation in Missouri, but John Henry's future would turn out quite differently! He always told people that he was born with a hammer in his hands. That might have just been an exaggeration of the truth! But ever since his earliest memories, John Henry loved swinging a hammer more than anything else. He was big and strong for his age, and as soon as he was able, he carried around one of his father's hammers. All day long he practiced swinging that hammer, enjoying the feel of it in his hands.

The Civil War began between the North and the South. Railroads were being built quickly, in order to help carry soldiers and supplies to the armies. John Henry would lie in his bed at night and listen to the far away whistles of the trains as they roared down the tracks. The whistles sounded exciting, as if they were calling out to him to come and join them. One day, a man from the North showed up at the plantation. He said that he had an important message for all of the slaves. The war had ended, and there was no more slavery. They were all free to do as they pleased!

There was no doubt in John Henry's mind about what he wanted to do! After all, he was born with a hammer in his hand. He kissed his parents good-bye and started walking until he reached the railroad tracks. He followed those tracks until he could hear the sound of workers in the distance. Quickly he went up to the foreman, who was in charge, and asked to be hired. As soon as the foreman saw how powerfully John Henry could swing a hammer, he offered him the job on the spot! John Henry had never felt as happy as he did at that moment. Every day he swung large, heavy hammers into steel spikes. He worked cheerfully for ten hours a day, singing out loud as he worked. People came to watch him work, amazed by his strength and speed.

One day John Henry was working with a team of men to drill a tunnel through a huge mountain made of solid rock. He swung his hammer as hard as he could, driving spikes into the rocks. Other men would follow behind, poking explosive black powder into the holes he had drilled. They would light the powder with a fuse, and then chunks of the mountain would blow up, forming holes that would become the tunnel. The foreman was standing nearby and watching John Henry work. Soon, a salesman appeared and said that he had a steam drill for sale that could dig faster than a whole team of men. The foreman was not convinced, saying that John Henry could dig as fast as any machine. The salesman offered a race between his drill and John Henry. Whoever could dig the farthest before the sun went down the next day would be the winner.

When the sun came up the next morning, John Henry was ready with his hammer in his hands. He said that he would win this race or he would die trying. He swung and swung, hitting those spikes harder than he ever had before. When he heard that the machine was ahead, he called out for another hammer. Holding two hammers at the same time, one in each arm, he went on swinging. Sparks flew as the hammer pounded into the spikes. On and on he swung, until at long last the sun's rays dipped down behind the horizon. The judges measured how far had been dug. John Henry had won by four feet! Amidst the cheers and congratulations, John Henry lay down on his back to rest, with a smile on his face. He opened his mouth and said proudly, "I was a steel driving man, born with a hammer in my hand." He closed his eyes, and never opened them again.

Review Questions:

1. What was John Henry born holding in his hand?
2. How did John Henry die?

Stormalong

Another one of America's "larger than life" folk heroes is Stormalong. Stormalong was born near the ocean in Massachusetts. He loved the sea from the day he was born. All day long, he would breathe in the salty sea spray until the blood in his veins turned into ocean water. He gazed and gazed out at the waves until his brown eyes changed color to become the blue-gray shade of the water. He knew there was nothing he wanted so badly as to be a sailor.

At ten years old, he was already two fathoms high. A fathom was six feet, which is the height of a tall grown man. So, he was as tall as two men standing on top of each other. His mother kept a ladder handy in the home so that she could climb up and give him a kiss whenever she wanted. One day, he decided to head to the city of Boston, where there were many big ships in the harbor. His mother packed up all the food she could find in the house and kissed him good-bye.

In Boston, Stormalong found a ship bound for China, named *Silver Maid*. He signed up to join the crew as a boat boy. His size did cause some problems at first. He learned that he had better not stand too close to the ship's rail, or he might tip the ship over by his weight. All of the sailors slept in hammocks, but there was no hammock that was even halfway big enough for Stormalong. He had to sleep in an extra large lifeboat every night! Soon, he realized that he would just have to go hungry, because if he ate all the food that his large body required, the ship's entire food supply would be gone before they reached China. Nevertheless, Stormalong found that he had been right about his love for sailing. He had never been happier than he was on the ocean!

That is, until the ship suddenly lurched and came to a complete stop one day in the middle of the water. The men's faces became pale with fear as they told Stormalong that they had been caught by a sea-monster called a *kraken*. Stormalong had never heard of such a creature before, but offered to dive overboard and find out what was the problem. Armed with his knife, he jumped into the deep water and swam under until he found that a giant sea-monster with many arms had indeed grabbed onto the Silver Maid. His knife proved useless against the strong creature, but Stormalong had another idea. He took each arm, one at a time, and tied it into a firm sailor's knot. Soon the arms were all tied up and the helpless monster sank to the ocean floor. Stormalong climbed back on board the ship, and was greeted as a hero!

After the voyage was completed, Stormalong decided that there was no ship big enough for his massive size. He began to build his own boat, called the Courser. The Courser was so huge that it took whole forests of trees to produce enough wood to build it. Once it was finished, Stormalong took it to the Arctic, where the best whaling grounds were. Americans liked to use whale bones to make things like needles and corsets. It was normally very dangerous and difficult to catch a whale, but Stormalong was so big and so strong that he could throw a harpoon into a whale easily. He only took the very largest ones that he caught, setting the smaller whales free. When his ship approached large icebergs, Stormalong simply shoved them out of the way with his hands. Soon Stormalong became known all over the country as a great hero of the seas!

Review Questions:

1. What did Stormalong love to do more than anything else?
2. What did Stormalong hunt in the Arctic waters?

Adventures in America Week 34

	Day 1	Day 2	Day 3
Reading	Read *Davy Crockett*	Read *Pecos Bill*	Read *Smart About* pg.10 and 9
Coloring/ Activity	Coloring Page, pg. 163	"Possibles Bag" activity	Color Arizona and Alaska on blank US map, pg. 2
Notebook	Narration from Read Aloud, history or reader, pg. 164	Copywork, pg. 165	Fill out notebook page for Arizona and Alaska, pgs. 166, 167

Optional Read-Aloud:

In Grandma's Attic
- Day 1: Chapter 7
- Day 2: Chapter 8
- Day 3: Chapter 9
- Day 4: Chapter 10
- Day 5: Chapter 11

Related Picture Books:

- *A Picture Book of Davy Crockett*, by David A. Adler

Possible Reader:

- *Prairie School*, Avi

Optional Copywork: Pecos Bill kept riding the tornado through state after state, watering the land.

Activity: Possibles Bag
You never know what you might end up needing when you are out on the open range. People used to carry with them a possibles bag that held various items that might become necessary.

Materials:
-Large brown paper bag   -Hole punch
-Yarn or leather string   -Scissors

•Cut out two large rectangles from the bag, trimming them to the same size.

•Use a hole punch to place holes up and down three sides of the rectangles, about one inch apart. Try to put the holes in the same places on each rectangle!

•Let your student lace through the holes with a piece of leather string or yarn. Tie off the ends at the top.

•Punch one hole in the center of each side at the top of the bag. Tie a long piece of yarn or leather through the holes to be a shoulder strap.

•Fill with some little practical items. (Small pack of tissue, mini flashlight, band aids, etc.)

•Now your child can be prepared for whatever "possibles" may come while traveling on the open range!

Notes

Davy Crockett

Davy Crockett was indeed a real person who actually fought and died in the Battle of the Alamo. The true story of his life is pretty amazing and almost unbelievable. It is easy to see how so much legend has grown up around him. Here are some of the facts and the legends about the "King of the Wild Frontier."

Davy Crockett learned to hunt around his home in Virginia when he was just eight years old. He always wore a coonskin hat made from the fur of a raccoon he had killed. The other animals all trembled and hid whenever he came through the woods. His special musket gun, named "Old Betsy," got just about everything he aimed for. Hunting bears was his specialty, but he also liked going after wolves, panthers and the occasional deer. Besides his incredible hunting skills, Davy was also a fabulous storyteller. Wherever he went, he made lots of friends because everyone thought he was so funny.

Davy Crockett's supreme knowledge of the land and his skill with a rifle soon led him to the army. There was a war between the white settlers and the Creek Indians, and the army wanted Davy Crockett to be in charge of the fighting. The war lasted longer than anyone had planned and eventually the army was out of food. Their barrels were practically empty and the men became afraid they might starve. In fact, they most likely would have starved if they had not had Davy Crockett there to take care of them. No matter where they were, he could always find animals to hunt. As often as the men were hungry, Davy went out and hunted enough wild game to feed them. This and his funny jokes made him very popular in the army.

Eventually Davy Crockett was married and moved his wife into a little log cabin in the woods. As soon as other settlers moved near, the Crocketts packed their things and went farther into the western frontier. Everyone liked Davy Crockett so much that they decided he should be in congress and help make laws that would be good for the people. He did that for a time, but missed living in the wild frontier. The Southern states were becoming crowded, so he went to live in Texas. At that time, Texas was actually part of Mexico! It was nice being there, but he and other American settlers did not really like living under Mexico's government and decided they would rather make their own rules. When the president of Mexico heard about that, he ordered an army to go stop them. The settlers hunkered down in a fort called the Alamo to keep safe. There was fierce fighting all around, and that was the last of Davy Crockett. He fought and died bravely with Old Betsy in his hands.

Review Questions:

1. What were some skills that Davy Crockett had?
2. Where was Davy Crockett when he died?

Pecos Bill

**The unbelievable character of Pecos Bill is a wonderful example of an American Tall Tale at its finest! Stories surrounding him are imaginative and creative, even if they are completely fictional.

From the time of his birth, Pecos Bill was unique. His mother soon discovered that feeding him ordinary milk was not going to work, so she had to go take milk from a mama mountain lion instead. Although he had over a dozen brothers and sisters as playmates, Bill's father felt that they were not quite his match. So, when Bill was two weeks old, his dad brought home a half grown bear cub. Frightened and confused, the cub growled and tried to bite little Bill. Indignant, Bill then tossed the bear up in the air a few times and wrestled it until the cub knew who was boss. Bill grew to love other creatures as well. Once he tried to make friends with a skunk. The skunk had different ideas. It lifted its tail and gave a good spray. Poor Bill's mother had to hang him up on the clothesline for a week to get the awful smell off of him!

By the time he was one year old, his family decided that their corner of Texas was becoming too crowded. They packed all their belongings and children into a covered wagon and headed out farther west. As the wagon jostled around over the rocks on the ground, little Bill lost his hold and was bounced right out of the wagon. His family did not see him fall so they just kept driving. Bill looked around and saw a pack of coyotes nearby. The coyotes had never seen a human baby before and thought he must be a little animal that had lost its fur. Bill decided to live with the coyotes, who taught him how to hunt prey and howl at the moon.

At ten years old, Bill still thought he was a coyote himself. One day a cowboy chanced upon him and was understandably shocked to see a naked boy howling and growling. He tried to talk to Bill, but since Bill could not understand human language, it was hard to communicate. The cowboy stayed for three days, teaching him how to talk. Finally he was able to convince Bill that he was really a human, so Bill bade the coyotes farewell and agreed to travel on with the cowboy.

They rode to a ranch, where Bill quickly took over as leader. No cowboy was as strong, brave or talented as Pecos Bill. He taught them how to lasso cattle. They preferred using rope although Pecos Bill always used a rattlesnake. He also taught them cowboy songs and just about everything else that cowboys know today.

There was a drought in the land because no rain had fallen for months. Suddenly a humongous black tornado came raging along. This gave Pecos Bill an idea. He rode his horse right up to the tornado and jumped on its back, squeezing the tornado's neck until all the water inside the clouds fell like buckets onto the parched earth. Pecos Bill kept riding the tornado through state after state, watering the land. After that, Pecos Bill was a famous hero and everyone loved him!

Review Questions:

1. What was unique or different about Pecos Bill's upbringing?
2. Tell me something interesting about Pecos Bill.

Adventures in America Week 35

	Day 1	Day 2	Day 3
Reading	Read *Paul Bunyan*	Read *Johnny Appleseed*	Read *Smart About* pg.18
Coloring/ Activity	Coloring Page, pg. 169	"Appleseed Print" activity	Color Hawaii on blank US map, pg. 2
Notebook	Narration from Read Aloud, history or reader, pg. 170	Copywork, pg. 171	Fill out notebook page for Hawaii, pg. 172

Optional Read-Aloud:

In Grandma's Attic
- Day 1: Chapter 12
- Day 2: Chapter 13
- Day 3: Chapter 14
- Day 4: Chapter 15
- Day 5: Chapter 16

Related Picture Books:
- *Paul Bunyan,* by Steven Kellogg

Possible Reader:
- *Clara and the Bookwagon,* Levinson

Activity: Appleseed Print

Materials:
-One apple   -Red tempura paint
-White paper

•Slice the apple in half, horizontally, so you can see the "star" of seeds in the center.

•Carefully remove the seeds.

•Pour some red paint onto a paper plate.

•Dip the cut side of one of the apple halves into the paint.

•Press the painted side of the apple onto the paper. You should be able to see the star visible in the middle of the print.

•Once the paint is dry, glue the apple seeds into the space in the middle of the star.

Optional Copywork: Paul Bunyan was the largest baby ever born in Maine.

Notes

Paul Bunyan

There are many stories and legends about men and women who helped to make America what it is today. Some of these are called Tall Tales because the truth was stretched over time. Most of these legends are about real people who actually lived, although they may not have done what the stories say they did. However, some of these legends were simply made up for fun and inspiration. Paul Bunyan is a character that most likely never existed, but it is still nice to imagine his adventures! There are many tales surrounding his life, but here are just a few.

Paul Bunyan was the largest baby ever born in Maine. Even as a baby, he had incredible strength. As soon as he was able to clap and laugh, the noise he made broke every window in his parents' house. Every time he rolled over, he destroyed everything in his path. His enormous size caused his parents so many problems that eventually they had to anchor his cradle out in the ocean. Not being on land didn't stop his ability to make trouble! He rocked his cradle so hard that humongous tidal waves flooded the town. Finally, his parents moved out into the wilderness where he could not bother anyone.

In the woods, Paul became great friends with all the wild animals. Bears were as tame as gentle kittens next to him. He grew immensely tall and was stronger than any man. One day, as he was out walking in a blue snowstorm, he ran into a mountain. He pushed against the mountain and discovered that it was actually an ox calf buried under a heap of blue snow. Paul adopted the ox and named her Babe. She grew to be exceptionally huge and never lost the blue color from the snow.

Once Paul had grown up, he took Babe and some friends out to clear the woods of the Midwest. He could cut down sixteen trees with one swoop of his axe. He was so hungry every day that it took quite an effort by his men to feed him. They built a humongous griddle which the men greased with slabs of bacon tied to their snowshoes. Then the cook would need the help of seven other men in order to flip pancakes fast enough. One time a woman entered his kitchen and asked the cook why there was such a tall pile of large logs stacked up inside. The cook answered that, "Those were no logs; they were sausages to go with Paul's pancakes for breakfast!"

Babe required a lot of water to drink, so Paul dug out the Great Lakes to be a water bowl for her. They traveled farther west. It became so hot that Paul let his great axe fall and drag behind him, thus digging out the Grand Canyon. Finally, Paul and Babe retired to the northern land of Alaska, where his booming laughter is still heard to this day!

Review Questions:

1. Tell me something interesting about Paul Bunyan.
2. How does the legend of Paul Bunyan say that the Great Lakes were made?

Johnny Appleseed

John Chapman was born and raised on a small farm in Massachusetts. There were many interesting things on the farm, but John's favorite place was his father's apple orchard. He loved to watch the trees change from bare branches in the winter, to delicate apple blossoms in the spring, then fill out with bright green leaves throughout the summer, before finally dropping perfectly ripe, delicious apples in the fall. John loved the tart, sweet fragrance of apples almost as much as he enjoyed a nice cup of hot apple cider or a warm slice of apple pie.

Ever since he was young, travelers had often told his family about the vast, fertile lands to the west. He heard how crops were growing so big and strong in that rich black soil. With an apple in his hand, he imagined what it would be like to watch apple trees grow tall and sturdy in such good earth. When he was eighteen years old, he left home taking bags full of apple seeds with him. He told people to call him Johnny Appleseed.

Everywhere he went, he planted nurseries of apple trees. If people could not afford to pay him for the seeds, he said never mind, he would give them away for free. He did not care much about money and gave away most of what he had. His clothing was ragged and worn, and his feet were usually bare. He was a gentle man who cared deeply for animals. Never touching meat, he only ate berries and nuts that he gathered in the woods. Once during a snowstorm, he crawled into a hollow log to stay dry. The log, he soon discovered, was not empty as he had thought! A mother bear and her cub were also seeking shelter inside. Johnny Appleseed snuggled right in there and spent the night with them.

He always carried his Bible and books of religious teachings along on his journey. He traveled from house to house, telling stories to the children and teaching the Bible to adults. Many people let him sleep on their floors at night, after feeding him a good supper. Most of the time, he was all alone except for the wild animals he called his friends. He believed that God was taking care of him, and he tried to live by the Golden Rule and treat others as he wanted to be treated.

For nearly fifty years, Johnny Appleseed traveled the country, generously sowing seeds wherever he went. Because of him, Americans all over were able to enjoy hot apple cider, delicious apple pies, and the beauty of apple trees changing through the seasons. Just as the seeds grew into tall abundant trees, the kindness he sowed also helped a land grow into a strong country.

Review Questions:

1. What kind of a man was Johnny Appleseed?
2. What did Johnny Appleseed bring to the western frontier?

Adventures in America Week 36

	Day 1	**Day 2**	**Day 3**
Reading	Read a book from the library about your state, or look on the internet for information.	Read a book from the library about your state, or look on the internet for information.	Read a book from the library about your state, or look on the internet for information.
Coloring/ Activity	Color the State Bird and Flower	Color the State Flag and Label the Capital on an Outline Map	**Celebrate the end of your year with a party!** Showcase your work to grandparents or friends.
Notebook	Narration from Read Aloud, state or reader, pg. 173	Copywork, pg. 174	Fill out notebook page for My State, assemble poster or lapbook, pg. 175

Optional Read-Aloud:

In Grandma's Attic
- Day 1: Chapter 17
- Day 2: Chapter 18
- Day 3: Chapter 19
- Day 4: Chapter 20
- Day 5: Chapter 21

Possible Reader:

- *Clara and the Bookwagon,* Levinson

Note This week you will focus on your own special state. If possible, find a book from the library about your home state, or find some pictures on the internet. You can make a poster or lapbook displaying the information. Include:
- Map outline of state, with capital labeled
- State bird
- State flower
- State motto
- State nickname
- Physical features (mountains, coasts, deserts, forests, prairies, etc.)
- Other interesting information (wildlife, history, famous attractions, etc)

Helpful websites for My State project:

http://www.coloringcastle.com/state_coloring_pages.html (This site has printable outline maps, with or without the capitals)

http://www.usa-printables.com/50_States (For illustrated maps and state flags)

http://www.kidzone.ws/geography/usa/alabama/flicker2.htm (For state birds and flowers)

http://www.socialstudiesforkids.com/usstates/50states.htm (Fun click and learn about each state)

Optional Copywork: This week, you can use your state's motto as copywork.

Notes

Star Spangled Banner

Oh, say can you see by the dawn's early light
What so proudly we hailed at the twilight's last gleaming?
Whose broad stripes and bright stars thru the perilous fight,
O'er the ramparts we watched were so gallantly streaming?
And the rocket's red glare, the bombs bursting in air,
Gave proof through the night that our flag was still there.
Oh, say does that star-spangled banner yet wave
O'er the land of the free and the home of the brave?

The Gettysburg Address

"Four score and seven years ago our fathers brought forth on this continent a new nation, conceived in liberty, and dedicated to the proposition that all men are created equal.

Now we are engaged in a great civil war, testing whether that nation, or any nation, so conceived and so dedicated, can long endure. We are met on a great battle-field of that war. We have come to dedicate a portion of that field, as a final resting place for those who here gave their lives that that nation might live. It is altogether fitting and proper that we should do this.

But, in a larger sense, we cannot dedicate, we cannot consecrate, we cannot hallow this ground. The brave men, living and dead, who struggled here, have consecrated it, far above our poor power to add or detract. The world will little note, nor long remember what we say here, but it can never forget what they did here. It is for us the living, rather, to be dedicated here to the unfinished work which they who fought here have thus far so nobly advanced. It is rather for us to be here dedicated to the great task remaining before us—that from these honored dead we take increased devotion to that cause for which they gave the last full measure of devotion—that we here highly resolve that these dead shall not have died in vain—that this nation, under God, shall have a new birth of freedom—and that government of the people, by the people, for the people, shall not perish from the earth."

Materials by Week

Week	Materials	Week	Materials
1	Flour, salt, water, oil, toothpick, paint, string	19	Paper lunch bag (white is best), cotton balls
2	Paper towel roll, construction paper	20	Any size wooden spoon, permanent markers or acrylic paint, optional: yarn, scraps of fabric
3	Large brown paper bag, brown, blue and green watercolor, black marker	21	White paper, white crayon, red & blue water color paint, ruler, masking tape
4	Black paper, white crayon, toothpick, flashlight	22	2 empty toilet paper rolls, construction paper, yarn or ribbon
5	Cardstock, construction paper, craft feathers	23	Brown paper grocery bag, 1 or 2 dark color markers
6	Empty egg carton, 2 toothpicks, white paper, either clay, play doughh or styrofoam	24	Empty pint size milk carton, white and brown construction paper, black cardstock
7	Yellow and green construction paper, popcorn	25	Sheet of white paper, vegetable oil, cotton ball
8	Vinegar, salt, sugar, cucumbers, onion	26	White, brown or black construction paper, googly eyes, yarn
9	Dried beans, small stones, bits of torn tissue, toy animals	27	2 handfuls stones and rocks, metallic gold paint, shallow pan, tub or sink
10	Paper	28	Cornmeal, salt, butter, whole milk, boiling water
11	Heavy whipping cream, clean jar, salt, optional: marble	29	Several colors of construction paper
12	Light blue construction paper, red, brown and green paint	30	Paper plate, 2 sheets black construction paper, 1 sheet black felt, black paint
13	Tin foil pie plate, thumbtack, old towel	31	3 c. soap flakes (Ivory Snow detergent or grate your own), vegetable oil, food coloring, bowl, water, 12 in. string
14	Flashlight	32	Stiff cardboard, metallic gold paint, nail or toothpick
15	Paper, marker, ribbon	33	Small lightweight hammer with wooden handle, acrylic paints
16	Red, white and blue paper	34	Large brown paper bag, hole punch, yarn or leather string
17	Salt, water, 3 c. any kind of berry, 100 % cotton white tee shirt	35	Apple, red tempura paint, white paper
18	Empty coffee can/ oatmeal canister, 2 sheets red construction paper, 1 sheet white or tan felt, rubber band, yarn, hole punch, 2 chopsticks or wooden dowels	36	Supplies for creating a lapbook (file folder) or a poster (poster board) plus printouts from internet of state map, flag, bird and flower

12239705R00083

Made in the USA
Monee, IL
23 September 2019